MUSIC
THE NEW LANGUAGE

by
WILLIAM F. LEE

ISBN 0-910957-65-7

9 780910 957656

TABLE OF CONTENTS

MUSIC IN THE 21st CENTURY:
THE NEW LANGUAGE

PRELUDE

This is a book about music and the music business. Unlike
other music books, it has no sharps and flats, no key signatures,
no meter signatures, no tempo indications, no phrase, breath,
nor bow markings, no libretti, no references nor terms relating
to the traditional study of music: historical, theoretical, bio-
graphical. It will introduce to you neither the basic fundamen-
tals nor the most esoteric literature. It will provide you with an
historical synopsis of the evolution of music and the music
business from ELECTRIC to ELECTRONIC and the vocabu-
lary with which to succeed in the field in the 21st century if
you plan to be, or are professionally involved in music as:

ARRANGER ARTIST REPRESENTATIVE BANDLEADER
COMPOSER CONDUCTOR CONTRACTOR
CRITIC DEPARTMENT DIRECTOR DIRECTOR
ENGINEER FACILITY MANAGER FILM SCORER
HARDWARE DESIGNER/MANUFACTURER
INSTRUMENT DESIGNER/MANUFACTURER
INVENTOR MUSIC ATTORNEY MUSIC HISTORIAN
MUSICOLOGIST PERFORMER PRODUCER
PROGRAMMER PROFESSOR PROMOTER PUBLICIST
PUBLISHER RESEARCHER SCHOOL DEAN
SOFTWARE DESIGNER/MANUFACTURER
STUDENT TEACHER
TELEVISION PRODUCER/DIRECTOR THEORIST

THE CHANCES OF SURVIVAL IN THE 21ST CENTURY
AS A PROFESSIONAL IN THESE FIELDS WITHOUT THE
UNDERSTANDING OF THE NEW LANGUAGE IN THIS
BOOK ARE MINIMAL!

Consider, it has only been possible to study music seriously in
the United States for a little over 100 years (New England
Conservatory, 1867). Since most of the immigrants originally
had come from Western Europe, the music we studied reflected
the traditions of those countries, primarily, Italy, Austria,
Germany, England, France, Spain, Poland, Finland, etc.
Virtually 100% of the music we heard was acoustically produced and acoustically transmitted since gramophone products
were not readily available commercially until around 1900 and
music making was limited to voices, harpsichords, pianos,
organs, strings, woodwinds, brasses, and percussion.
Conservatory and university music curricula were formulated
to accommodate this history, and composers emulated, for the
most part, the Western European tradition with some experi-
mentation and alteration of the twelve semi-tone, serial, octave
tradition.

All the while, the nature of the world and music began to
change and evolve. Wars, transportation and communication
made serious inroads in demographics, education, and venues
of enlightenment and entertainment. The United States was
becoming a major contender as we left the ROMANTIC
PERIOD and entered the SCIENTIFIC PERIOD. Electricity,
which had made an enormous impact on the quality of life in

America during the first half of the 20th century, was bringing about serious changes in the kind and amount of music being heard as the number of available commercial phonograph recordings was escalating and the establishment of the first AM radio station (KDKA, 1920) brought a new wave of aural availability. Jazz was developing into America's "serious music" and being received warmly throughout the world. All of this notwithstanding, it has only been possible to study this art form as a major endeavor for fewer than 40 years!

As we entered the second half of the 20th century electricity/electronics began to have its impact. The refinement of the electric guitar, electric bass, electric/electronic keyboards, the 33 1/3 long-playing record, computers, the development of FM radio, the transistor, television, the eight-track, synthesizers, the cassette, CD's, artificial intelligence, advanced telecommunication, the movies, jingles, MIDI, all contributed to the rapid acceleration toward the 21st century. Acoustic sounds began to make way for more and better recordings, stereo TV, superb sound reinforcement at most live concerts, and more and more use of electronic instruments. The professional concert bands that once occupied the gazebos in the parks disappeared. The big swing/jazz bands disappeared. More and more choral activities were disappearing from the professional ranks and shifting to amateur events, primarily in the churches. Eight to twelve-piece acoustic lounge and club-date bands were diminishing to one, two, and three-piece electronic group(s); the number of symphony orchestras were growing at the part-time, amateur level to provide performance outlets for the thousands of acoustically trained musicians from our schools and colleges who had to seek full-time employment in other fields.

Many of the music magazines and journals which educated us e.g., AMERICAN ORGANIST, ETUDE, JAZZ REVIEW, KEYNOTE, METRONOME, MODERN MUSIC, MUSIC & MUSICIANS, MUSIC FORUM, MUSIC WORLD, MUSICAL CLARION, MUSICAL COURIER, RECORD CHANGER, were now defunct. The vacant shelves they left were filled with state-of-the-art periodicals, e.g., COMPUTER MUSIC JOURNAL, ELECTRONIC INDUSTRY WEEKLY, ELEC-TRONIC MEDIA, ELECTRONIC MUSICIAN, ELECTRONIC MUSIC REVIEW, ELECTRONOTES, KEYBOARD MAGA-ZINE, MCS: MUSIC, COMPUTERS & SOFTWARE, MUSIC BUSINESS CONTACTS, MUSIC TECHNOLOGY, NEW MUSIC, and POLYPHONY: ELECTRONIC MUSIC & HOME RECORDING.

Professionals in music and music-related fields in the future must be knowledgeable in computers (hardware and software), synthesizers, samplers, and controllers, analog and digital, MIDI, film editing and the technical language as it relates to their use. That technical language is defined, term by term, in The New Language section of this book. THIS IS NOT THE END, JUST THE BEGINNING!

THE NEW LANGUAGE

Aa

A/Q comparison - A way of comparing two signals.

AC - *See* **Alternating current**.

AC adapter - *See* **Battery eliminator.**

Access - Find. Access an item of information.

AC coupling - A way of interconnecting stages in an electronic circuit.

Acoustics - The science dealing with sound and the treatment thereof.

Active circuitry - A powered circuit, such as a synthesizer, electronic piano or studio mixer. Also a component included in some electric guitars and basses, enabling wider frequency control and boosting more facilities than are available in passive instruments.

Active sensing - A MIDI message sent by some instruments which instructs receiving instruments to shut off during performance in the event that a MIDI cable is disconnected.

AD - Attack/Decay. One of the simplest types of envelope generators.

ADC - Analog to Digital Converter. A device which takes in analog (electrical) information and converts it to numeric (digital) information. In music computers, the device which takes input from a keyboard (or other analog sound source) and converts it into information the computer can store.

A/D converter - This device converts analog information to digital form. *See* **Analog to digital converter.**

Additive synthesis - The combining of two or more audio waveforms to create a more complex sound. This may be done to add harmonics to a fundamental tone or to create a dissonant mixture rich in special effects and overtones. *See* **Subtractive synthesis.**

Address - Each location in a computer memory is numbered consecutively. The number is referred to as the location's address.

ADR - Automatic Dialogue Replacement. An electronic device used in video post production for looping of badly recorded dialogue.

ADSR - An acronym for Attack, Decay, Sustain and Release, referring to the dynamic characteristics common to all sounds. In an analog synthesizer the ADSR control provides control over these parameters and considerable sound modifying possibilities.

AES - Audio Engineering Society.

Aftertouch - A type of touch sensitivity in which the keyboard senses how hard the key is being pressed down after it has reached and is resting on the keyboard. Monophonic and polyphonic aftertouch are defined separately in each MIDI specification.

AGC - Automatic gain control.

AI - Artificial Intelligence. Simulating human thought processes, to solve problems through the use of a computer.

Algorithm - An algorithm is a plan for solving a problem. It consists of a sequence of distinct, well-defined steps. Following the algorithm will always produce an answer in a finite number of steps. Also, different operator configurations used in Yamaha's FM sound generating system.

Algorithmic composition - Composing music with a computer which has been programmed to the rules of an algorithm, compositional method of style.

Alias frequency - An erroneous frequency created when sampling a signal whose frequency is higher than the Nyquist frequency.

Aliasing - The creation of erroneous, or "alias" frequencies.

Alkaline battery - Used for effects boxes, guitar preamps, etc. A long-lasting battery.

All-notes-off - A MIDI command, recognized by some synthesizers and other sound-generating modules, which causes any notes that are currently sounding to be shut off.

Allpass - A filter that passes all audio frequencies, keeping them at their levels, while introducing phase shift into the signal.

Alpha copy - *See* **Alpha unit.**

Alpha dial - A control that selects a parameter to be edited which was made popular by Roland.

Alphanumeric - A combination of alphabetic and numeric, meaning both letters and numbers.

Alpha unit - The name given a product which is tested on-site prior to approving it for beta test sites.

Alternating current (AC) - As opposed to direct current (DC), electricity whose direction of current flow reverses regularly between positive and negative.

ALU - Arithmatic and Logic Unit. Part of a central processor that actually executes the operations requested by an input command.

AM - *See* **Amplitude modulation.**

Ambience - The acoustic characteristics of a room or area with regard to reverberation. A room with a lot of reverberation is said to be "live", one without is "dead".

Amp - Amplifier or Ampere.

Ampere - A unit of electrical current.

Amplifier - An instrument used to expand or increase the power of sound or signal.

Amplitude - The loudness of a sound. In electronic music, the maximum value of a waveform from the center of its periodic cycle, which is a function of amounts of AC voltage.

Amplitude modulation (AM) - The use of a control voltage to alter (or modulate) the loudness of an audio signal. This control voltage may come from another audio generator or voltage-controlled amplifier to affect the attack and decay characteristics of a waveform.

AM synthesis - A method of synthesis based on alteration of the amplitude of a signal.

Analog - There are two main ways of doing things electronically. In the analog method, signals are continuously variable and the slightest change may be significant. Analog circuits are subject to drift, distortion, and noise, but they are capable of handling complex signals with relatively simple circuitry. Traditional electronic musical instruments and synthesizers (1900 to present) have used analog techniques but microprocessor-based systems employ digital synthesis.

Analog delay - An electronic device for delaying a signal by using "bucket brigade" integrated circuitry, and may also be obtained by using a tape machine. *See* **Tape echo.**

Analog/digital converter - A device that samples an analog signal and transforms it into a digital representation of that signal.

Analog/digital hybrid - A sampler or synthesizer that makes use of analog and digital technology, usually in the form of analog tone-generating or tone-shaping circuitry combined with digital tone-generating circuitry or digital control circuitry.

Analog sequencer - A sequencer in which the control voltages to be played back are specified mechanically using a bank of analog pots rather than stored in digital memory.

Analog synthesis - Synthesis based on analog electronic technology.

Analog technology - Technology that generates or processes signals that are continuous.

Analog-to-digital conversion - The changing of analog signals to digital signals within a computer network.

Analog-to-digital converter - A device which converts (encodes) a quantitized analog level into a digital word.

Anti-aliasing filter - To prevent aliasing; a filter that restricts the frequency range of an audio signal.

Aperiodic - A singularly occurring wave characterized by random, irregular patterns.

Aperiodic waveform - An irregular, non-repeating waveform without pitch.

Application program - A software program that consists of coded instructions for the computer to follow. Application programs are usually distributed on floppy disks and are sometimes called software or software application programs.

Application software - Computer programs which carry out pragmatic chores, e.g., accounting, sequencing, word processing, etc.

AR - Attach-release envelope generator.

Arpeggiator - A device that automatically steps one at a time through a group of notes specified by keys which are held down or latched. Unlike a sequencer, an arpeggiator cannot usually play irregular rhythms or chords.

Artificial intelligence (AI) - Program that enable computers to play chess, prove theorems, recognize patterns, or do anything else which requires learning or reasoning.

ASCII - American Standard Code for Information Interchange. ASCII is a code for representing upper and lower case letters, numbers, symbols, and punctuation marks. It is the code used by most computers and terminals except IBM equipment.

ASIC - Application Specific Integrated Circuit. An integrated circuit dedicated to a specific application.

Assembler - A program which translates instructions written in assembly language into machine language.

Assembly language - A great help to the programmer which allows him to write a program using words like LOAD, JUMP, and CLR for instructions, instead of long strings of 1's and 0's.

Assignable - Capable of altered function. An "assignable" control may have several functions under the control of software.

Assigning - Also known as routing, a switching technique used with multitrack mixers whereby the engineer directs any input to any or all output channels. Normally all circuits are wired to a routing, or assigning, switch on the board.

Assignment - A term that is applicable to polyphonic synthesizers, referring to the determination as to which voice module is to be controlled by which note currently being played.

Assignment priority - The routing scheme in a polyphonic synthesizer that determines which key will activate which voice.

* Asterisk - Since most printing mechanisms lack a times sign, computer languages often use an asterisk to indicate multiplication. A times B = A * B.

Asynchronous - An operation which does not process in step with some external timing, but at its own pace.

Asynchroneous communications adaptor - A device attached to a computer to enable it to effect asynchronous communications over a telephone line.

Attack - *See* **Envelope**. *See* **Rise time.**

Attack velocity - The rate at which a key goes from the key UP to key DOWN position.

Attenuation - The process of reducing the amplitude of a signal.

Attenuator - A level control which may be switched or smoothly varied to reduce the gain of an electronic circuit. *See* **Potentiometer.**

Audio-cassette interface - A connection allowing ordinary cassette recorders to be connected to computers for the purpose of storing programs on cassette tapes.

Audio input - An input to a signal modifier that accepts the signal the modifier is intended to act on.

Audio taper potentiometer - A pot whose resistance changes at a logarithmic rate matching the human ear response.

Auto-correct - Also called quantization, a function found on most sequencers and drum machines, which causes notes played during real-time data entry to be assigned to the nearest available rhythmic value. Also called quantizing and time-correcting.

Auto-glide - A portamento in which there is a pitch slide between notes only when a new key is depressed while the previous key is still being held down. Also, fingered portamento.

Auto-locator - A trade name of the MCI Company, to describe their tape transport control system. *See* **SMPTE.**

Automation - The replacement of human labor with machines.

Auto-tune - A switch or button that causes an instrument to automatically tune its oscillators and other tunable circuits.

Azimuth - The angular relationship between the head gap and the tape path.

Azure noise - A random signal, weighted so that the higher frequencies are more pronounced.

Bb

B - Abbreviation for binary as used in programming notation.

Backup - A copy of a program or data file made as insurance, in the event the original gets lost or damaged. *See* **Working copy.**

Balance - The relative level of two or more instruments, signal paths, or recorded tracks.

Balanced line - A line consisting of two conductors plus a shield. With respect to ground, the conductors are at equal potential, but opposite polarity. *See* **Unbalanced line.**

Balanced modulator - A device that differs in circuit design but has the same audio effect as a ring modulator. *See* **Ring modulator.**

Band-pass filter - An electronic filter that allows only those sounds between specified high-and low-frequency cutoff points to be heard. A common component of synthesizers. *See* **Filter, band-pass.**

Band-reject filter - An electronic filter that allows only those sounds above or below specified high-and low-frequency cutoff points to be heard. A common component of synthesizers. *See* **Filter, band-reject.**

Bandwidth - The arithmetic difference between the upper and lower cut-off frequencies of an audio system. Frequency range.

Bank - A set of patches that can be called up with a related set of commands. Also, any related set of items, e.g., filter bank, etc.

Barber pole effect - *See* **Shepard function generator.**

BASIC - Beginner's All-purpose Symbolic Instruction Code. A programming language designed to be used from interactive terminals. BASIC is easy to learn and resembles a simplified FORTRAN. BASIC is the high level language most often supplied with small computers.

Basic channel - The channel over which voice and channel messages are sent in MIDI.

Basic Tracks - In multi-track recording, those tracks that are recorded first. In general, the rhythm tracks (guitars, bass, drums, keyboards, etc.).

Bass synthesizer - An electric bass synthesizer designed to work with an electric bass controller.

Battery eliminator - A device which converts AC voltage to a suitable voltage for replacing a battery.

Baud - A term used in describing data transmission rates; usually one bit per second. Named for the inventor of the original teletype code, Jean Maurice Emile Baudot.

B - A binary-based code that represents alphanumerics and a limited number of symbols with 5-bit characters.

BBS - Bulletin Board System. Designed for a computer and a modem to read messages that other people have left on the system, or to leave messages of your own.

BCD - Binary Coded Decimal. A system of representing decimal numbers digitally, e.g.:

0		0000
1		0001
2		0010
3		0011
4		0100
5		0101
6		0110
7		0111
8		1000
9		1001
10	0001	0000

Beat - The interaction caused by two closely related pitches sounding simultaneously. This interaction takes the form of a wavering in the loudness of the total sound, and is a useful means of tuning two pitches together.

Beats per minute - *See* **BPM**.

Bend - To change pitch in a sliding manner by use of a lever, pitch-band wheel, or ribbon.

Bernoulli bow - A storage device that holds a flexible disk in a square cartridge, suspended by air pressure while in use.

Beta - Sony's home videotape standard.

Beta Hi-Fi - Data with high sound quality.

Beta test site - The impartial test site which receives products approved by the alpha test site.

Beta unit - A software program or device which has been approved by the alpha test site.

Bias signal - A constant-level signal designed to optimize an electronic circuit's operation.

Bias voltage - A constant-level voltage designed to optimize a particular electronic circuit's operation.

Binary (B) - The number system that computers use is called binary. It uses only two digits, 1 and 0. This is because the electronic circuits used in the computer have only two states; on and off. These are the numbers zero to sixteen in binary:

0	00000
1	00001
2	00010
3	00011
4	00100
5	00101
6	00110
7	00111
8	01000

17

9	01001
10	01010
11	01011
12	01100
13	01101
14	01110
15	01111
16	10000

Binary numbering system - *See* **Numbering system, binary.**

BIOS - Basic Input/Output System - A computer system software that is hardware independent, and interfaces with computer elements.

Bipolar power supply - A power supply that generates positive and negative DC voltages.

Bipolar signal swing - A signal whose amplitude, with respect to ground, varies between positive and negative.

Bit - BInary digiT. The smallest possible unit of information. One bit is enough to tell the difference between yes or no, up or down, on or off, one or zero; any two opposites. Computers must represent information in the form of bits because the electronic circuits they are made of can have only two states: on or off.

Block diagram - A representation of a system, circuit, or program in which the individual functions are symbolized by labeled boxes and the relationships between them by connecting lines.

Bloom - When a CRT has its intensity set too high, it is said to "bloom." Also, the description of how a reverberant sound develops.

Blue noise - Pitchless, non-repetitive signal containing all audible frequencies with an increase in relative amplitude of the higher frequencies.

Board - *See* **Console.**

Bomb - A program "bombs" when it fails. A programmer "bombs" a computer system when he deliberately writes a program that will disrupt the system.

Boost/cut control - A control which cuts some parameter when rotated counterclockwise and boosts some parameter when rotated clockwise.

Boot - To start up a computer system with a bootstrap loader. A boot track on a disk is a built-in program which carries out the above procedure.

Bounce - When a pair of contacts meet in a switch, key, or relay, they do not remain closed. They spring apart and then back together several times before settling down. *See* **Debounce.**

BPM - Beats per minute.

Breakpoint - Some computers have a switch which will cause them to stop when coming upon a certain point in the program. The same effect can also be achieved by putting STOP instructions in the program. This is the break-point. Also, in Yamaha DX/TX synthesizers, the point of reference for an operator's keyboard level scaling curves.

Breath controller - A MIDI continuous controller code generated by a device that is sensitive to air pressure which is used by blowing into the device. It is generally used to produce modulation.

Brickwall filter - A lowpass filter noted for a response that stays almost constant until the cutoff frequency, then drops off past the cutoff point.

Bridge board - *See* **Emulator board.**

Bubble memory - Inside a slab of semi-magnetic material, tiny magnetized regions can be created and look like tiny bubbles. A memory device may be set up in a ring or series of rings which provide a way of sensing the presence or absence of a bubble. Bubble memories may become a non-moving-parts replacement for the floppy disk.

Buffer - A buffer is a temporary storage area for data. It is often used when data transmission must take place at differing speeds. In the hardware realm, a buffer is a device that amplifies a signal, giving it greater drive capability. For a MIDI recorder, a section of computer memory used to store sections of sequences during cut and paste operations.

Bug - A bug is an error in a program that keeps it from working properly. In recording, jargon for contact mike or pickup used on acoustic guitars, violins, saxophones, etc.

Bulletin board system - A communications system which allows for the sending and receiving of messages, accessed by a computer and a modem.

Burwens noise reduction system - Developed by the Burwens company, a method of single-ended noise reduction that employs a variable low-pass filter.

Bus - In electronics, a bus is a power line that provides power to a large number of circuits. In computing, a bus is a group of wires that conveys information to a large number of devices. The information may be data, commands, or addresses, or all three in sequence. Bus-oriented systems are popular because they are flexible and easy to expand.

Buss - *See* **Bus.**

Byte - Originally defined as a subdivision of a long computer word, byte has come to mean a piece of information 8 bits long. MIDI messages are sent on a series of bytes.

Cc

C - A computer language developed by Bell Labs for systems programming. C is terse and gives the programmer great freedom.

Cache - A section of RAM dedicated to holding the newest data from disk so that future use of this data does not require additional disk access.

Cache memory - A high-speed memory capable of keeping up with the CPU. It acts as a buffer between the CPU and the slower main memory.

CAD/CAM - Computer-Aided Design and Computer-Aided Manufacture. They consist of drafting aids used to lay out printed circuit boards and integrated circuit chips and the use of computers to manage and control a factory's operation.

CAI - Computer Aided Instruction. A method of drilling students and reinforcing lessons through question-and-answer dialogs with a computer.

CAM - Computer Aided Manufacturing. The application of computers to the manufacturing of products.

Camcorder - A recorder and video camera built into a hand-held, single piece of equipment.

Cancel - In computers, to stop a program which is running without saving the results produced.

Cannon connector - See **XLR connector.**

Capacitance - An opposition to a change in voltage.

Capacitance sensing - A touch sensitivity that senses the amount of key surface covered by a fingertip, and generates a corresponding generation of output voltage.

Capacitor - An electronic component that opposes a change in voltage. Parallel conductors in a signal line may take on the properties of a capacitor, thereby attenuating high frequencies.

Carbon-zinc battery - Inexpensive battery that is best for applications which require little current consumption.

Card - A circuit board that plugs into a slot in the computer which enables the computer to do more tasks.

Carrier - The tone that a modem hears when the modem at the other end of the line is listening, but not transmitting. Its disappearance means that the circuit has been broken. Also, an audio signal which is being modulated by some other signal, as in FM.

Cartridge - The removable section at the end of the tone arm of a record player which contains an electronic mechanism capable of transforming mechanical motion into electrical current. *See* **Electrical current**. Also, a plug-in memory storage device which may be either RAM or ROM, and are normally usable only on devices built by a single manufacturer.

Cartridge memory - A plug in package that is used to store data, usually voicing information. A cartridge will generally house some form of random access memory.

Cassette interface - A circuit that changes computer data into audio tones that then may be recorded on regular cassette tapes.

Cassette storage - Digital information about patch programs or sequencer or drum machine patterns stored on cassette tape.

Catalog - A DOS command to display the list of files present on a disk. Also called directory.

Cathode ray tube - *See* **CRT.**

CD - Compact Disc. An optical-based digital recording medium. CD's have a wide dynamic range, high signal-to-noise ratio, and a mimimun amount of wear.

CD-I - Compact Disc Interactive. Played on a special player that includes a computer, the CD-I system can store audio signals, stop motion video, software programs, text, and other digital data.

CD-ROM - Compact Disc ROM. Designed for computers which store the maximum amount of data, a read-only storage medium.

CD-S - Compact Disc Single. A small CD capable of storing less digital auto information than a regular CD.

CD-V - Compact Disc Video. A regular sized CD which is capable of storing five minutes of audio and video program material, and 20 minutes of additional audio.

Cell - A unit of memory in a computer. Also, a complete unit of information in a spreadsheet program.

Cent - The unit for the scientific measurement of intervals. A cent is one hundredth of a half tone = 100 cents, and an octave contains 1200 cents.

Center detent - A notch in the operation of a controller that allows the user to return the controller to its original postion.

Chain - An ordered series, e.g., a program chain, a set of patch programs; a song chain, in a drum machine, etc.

Channel - A single audio signal. In a console, the signal-processing path for such a signal. *See* **Tracks**. In MIDI, the 16 channels are numerical data designations, all of which share a single cable.

Channelize - Assigning MIDI data to a MIDI channel.

Channel key pressure - A MIDI message sent when a key is pressed down after it has been struck.

Channel message - A MIDI message that is only received by MIDI devices in a MIDI network which are set to the same MIDI channel as the sending device.

Channel mode messages - *See* **Mode messages.**

Channel pressure - A type of MIDI data that contains monophonic aftertouch information.

Channel voice messages - MIDI codes which represent actual music performance, e.g., aftertouch, continuous controllers, note on and off, pitch bend, and program changes.

Chapman Stick - Invented by Emmet Chapman in 1970, a 10-string music instrument with lower range than an electric bass and higher range than a guitar. It is played by tapping the strings with two hands.

Character - A small group of bits whose arrangement is given some definite meaning.

Chase lock - A process wherein a control unit monitors the timing signals sent by two devices, e.g., an audio tape recorder and a video tape recorder, synchronizes and locks the signals, and controls the speed of the master and slave.

Chip - Refers to the tiny bit of silicon that forms the heart of an integrated circuit, or else to the entire integrated circuit. Also known as microprocessor.

Chorus - An electronic device which creates the effect of more than one sound from a single source by combining a short delay (usually between 5 and 30 milliseconds) with slight deviations in pitch.

Chorusing - Signal processing that is a type of flanging which mixes a time-delayed signal with the original signal and modulates the length of the delay by an LFO, thereby changing the relative strengths and phase relationships of the overtones and creating a more animated sound.

Chrome tape - A tape whose formulation is based on chromium oxide, which provides greater high frequency headroom than ferric tape.

Circuit - A path made up of various connections and conductors through which electrical current flows.

Circuit board - A printed circuit with electronic components mounted on it and soldered in place.

Clamping -The limitation of a voltage to a specified level, e.g., when an oscillator receives a command pulse, the slave oscillator resets to whatever point in its cycle corresponds to the clamping level.

Clangorous - Containing partials that are not part of the normal harmonic series.

C language - A high level programming language used by factory software writers; now used as the main language in a major music-computer.

Classical electronic music studio - A studio for the composition of electronic music in which the primary consideration is tape manipulation through speed variation, editing, reverberation, loops, etc.

Click - When one of the switches on a computer's mouse is pressed to activate a function, it is called a click.

Click track - (1) A rhythmic guide track consisting of a series of clicks used to assist in time-keeping during recording; (2) clicks recorded in order to start or cue synthesizer sequences or electronic drums. The clicks can be used to trigger a number of different sequences recorded at different times while still keeping them all in synchronization.

Click track generator - An electronic metronome that makes time-keeping signals for a click track.

Clipping - The level of power where distortion takes hold in an amplifier.

Clock - This is the master source of the computer's timing pulses. Everything proceeds in step with them. Also, low-frequency pulse clock, audio-rate sync clock and other MIDI clock signals. Also, a stop-watch for use in recording sessions for film scores or jingles.

Clone - Any computer that is compatible with IBM PC software.

Close - To cease work on a particular computer data file, and return to the main menu or the operating system.

Closed architecture - *See* **Closed system.**

Closed-circuit mono phone jack - A jack that has hot, ground, and switching terminals.

Closed system - In order to maximize sales of their peripherals, some computer manufacturers use a computer design which makes it difficult to add peripherals designed by other manufacturers; thus, a "closed system".

Clustered devices - Terminals and printers connected to a common controller.

CMI - Computer-Managed Instruction. Akin to CAI, however, the computer is the primary teacher with secondary faculty guidance and tutoring.

CMOS - Complementary MOS. An extension of MOS technology which produces integrated circuits with very low power consumption.

Coarse tune - A control used for making large changes in the pitch of an oscillator, sometimes used with a fine-tune control.

Code - This can refer to a method of representing symbols in binary bits or to the lines of instructions making up a computer program. Also, any digitally-transmitted or recorded signal. MIDI is a code.

Cold start - A program's initial entry point. Here the program initializesthehardware, clears its buffers and workspaces, sets up pointers, and does all the other housekeeping it requires before getting down to serious business.

Colored noise - Sound which results when a filter is used to give emphasis to a particular band of the white noise spectrum.

Come up - Jargon for powering up a computer.

Command - An instruction from the computer user telling the computer to perform some action.

Command language - The set of commands that are valid for a particular system.

Command level - The ability to control a computer system via commands.

Command line interface - A way of communicating with a computer that involves the use of both numbers and letters.

Common Messages - *See* **System Common Messages**.

Compact Disc - *See* **CD**.

Compact Disc Read-Only Memory - *See* **CD-ROM.**

Compander - The contraction of COMpressor/exPANDER, often used in describing the action of a noise reduction system.

Compansion - A combination of COMpression/exPANSION. A noise reduction method.

Compansion ratio - In a compansion system, the compression ratio and expansion ratio.

Comparator - In digital, a circuit that compares two numeric values and indicates at its output if they are the same or different. In analog, a circuit which compares its input signal to a predetermined threshold, therefore indicating when the threshold has been exceeded.

Compatible - The ability of software and hardware to perform together.

Compiler - The compiler provides one of the ways of implementing a high-level language. The compiler is a program that translates each command into a series of instructions in machine language.

Complementary - metal-oxide semi-conductor -*See* **CMOS.**

Complementary signal processing - A signal processing technique, in which some processing is done before recording, with equal-and-opposite (complementary) processing during playback. Examples are noise reduction systems and tape recorder pre-and post-emphasis. *See* **Non-complementary signal processing.**

Compressor - An electronic device for reducing the range of dynamics of an audio signal. As its input level is increased, its gain decreases.

Computer - A device which manipulates data according to a series of instructions stored in its memory. While the individual operations performed by the electronic computer are simple, it does them at the rate of thousands per second, enabling complex tasks to be finished in a short time. Most computers used with MIDI are personal computers (PC'S).

Computer-aided design - *See* **CAD.**

Computer-aided instruction - *See* **CAI.**

Computer interface - A device that allows a computer to talk to another device.

Computer literacy - An understanding of computers and how to apply them to the solution of problems.

Computer music - Music created with aid of a computer. Types of computer music include (1) that in which the computer helps compose written music for performance by traditional, nonelectronic instruments; (2) that which is composed using a computer and is generated directly by the system through the digital-to-analog conversion of stored information into amplified sound; (3) that generated by an analog synthesizer with the computer providing control-voltage inputs and instructions; (4) the analog-to-digital conversion of sounds coming from analog sources such as synthesizers, microphones, and magnetic pickups, which are manipulated using a computer and then presented through the digital-to-analog conversion of the DIGITIZED sound; and (5) the interaction of musicians and computers that are programmed to respond to audio input in a real-time setting.

Computer science - The art of solving problems with computers.

Computer synthesis - As applies to music, applications in which the choice of notes and related attributes has been determined to a significant degree by means of the computer. One of the earliest uses of the computer as a tool for composition was at the University of Illinois in 1955 by Lejaren Hiller and Leonard Isaacson.

Concurrent DOS - Identified with Digital Research, a disk operating system which allows for multi-user and multi-tasking operation.

Condenser microphone - *See* **Microphone, condenser.**

Conductor - Any material which has low resistance to electrical current flow.

Configure - To set up for use. Also, to adjust software and/or hardware to make them compatible.

Console - A panel containing the indicator lights, switches, and video screens needed by the operator to control the computer and monitor its operation. In recording, the piece of equipment through which inputs and outputs are routed either to or from a tape recorder, and with which adjustments in tone, level and balance are made. It is also known as a board, desk, or mixing console.

Constant voltage transformer - A transformer which controls variations in input voltage to allow for a constant voltage.

Continue - The MIDI code that instructs a drum machine or sequencer to play from the last stopping point.

Continuous controllers - Modulation wheels, breath controllers, and any of the MIDI codes created by moving levers, pedals, sliders, or wheels.

Continuous duty - The maximum time that a device can be operative.

Contour - *See* **Envelope**.

Contour amount - A control which regulates the amount of envelope voltage that enters the VCF or VCA.

Contour generator - *See* **Envelope generator**.

Control change - MIDI messages created by continuous controllers, pedals, or switches.

Control input - An input on a synthesizer that will accept a control voltage to activate and modulate such components as oscillators, amplifiers, and filters.

Controller - Circuitry that governs the operation of a device. *See* **Manual controller, Sequential controller, Linear controller, Keyboard controller.**

Controller #7 - *See* **MIDI volume.**

Control voltage - The electrical signal which, in an analog synthesizer, specifies which frequency is played by the oscillators. Also, a voltage produced by a controller, e.g., envelope generator, keyboard, modulation wheel, etc.

Co-processor - To achieve more system efficiency, a microprocessor that works in tandem with another microprocessor.

Copy protection - To reduce unauthorized copying of programs, some software publishers often use tricks to make disks difficult to copy, therefore prohibiting legitimate users from making backups.

Cosine wave - A waveform of identical shape to a sine wave, but 90 degrees out of phase with it.

CP/M - Control Program for Micro-processors. CP/M is an early DOS written for small computers using the 8080 family of micro-processors.

Cps - Characters per second. Relating to data transmission.

CPS - Cycles per second.

CPU - Central Processing Unit. It contains all the registers, arithmetic circuitry, comparators, etc., that do the work of computing.

CPUID - Found only on mainframe computers, an identification number that identifies the CPU in a machine-readable format.

Crash - A computer system crashes when it stops working for some reason and must be restarted by the operator. *See* **Bomb.**

Cross-fade looping - In some digital samplers, a feature in which some portion of the end of a loop is mixed with some portion of the beginning of the same loop which produces a smoother loop.

Cross-modulation - A type of patch in which one of the audio oscillators in each voice is being modulated by another, or by an envelope generator.

Crosstalk - In a signal path, the unwanted detection of a signal from an adjacent signal path.

CRT - Cathode Ray Tube. The technical name of the picture tube in a TV set or video terminal.

C-60 - Audio cassette tape with 30 minutes on each side, as opposed to C-30 with 15 minutes on each side, and C-90 with 45 minutes per side.

C-64 - Commodore-64. A home computer.

Cue - Also known as talkback, part of the circuitry of the mixing console which enables: (1) the engineer in the control room and the musicians in the studio to communicate via headphones; (2) previously recorded material to be fed to the musicians so that they can play in sync when doing overdubs; and (3) direct injection instruments to be monitored via headphones while recording is in progress.

Cue list - Usually related to SMPTE or MIDI Time Code, the chronological order in which events need to be initiated.

Current consumption - Usually specified in amperes, milliamperes, or microamperes, the amount of current drawn by a device.

Cursor - A mark that a video terminal makes on its screen which indicates the direction of the next character.

Cut - A technique in which one segment of film is spliced directly to another, creating an immediate change of subject or view, in film music. Also, to remove data.

Cut and paste - To temporarily remove data for storage in a buffer, to be used later. In a MIDI recorder or music notation program, features that allow for marking a section of a sequence or a score, duplicate it, move it to a new location, or remove it from the sequence.

Cut-off frequency - In a high-pass or low-pass filter, the frequency at which the output level has fallen by 3 dB. On most synthesizers, the cutoff frequency is both manually adjustable and voltage-controllable.

CV - Control Voltage. A signal that instructs voltage controlled devices. *See* **Control voltage.**

CV/GATE - Input for triggering an analog synthesizer.

Cybernetics - The study of communication and control in natural and artificial information handling systems.

Cylinder - A cylinder is composed of all the corresponding tracks on a set of disks. There are as many concentric cylinders as there are tracks on one disk. Inasmuch as the read/write heads for the disks move in unison, they look at all the tracks of a particular cylinder at once.

Dd

DAC - *See* D/A conversion.

D/A conversion - Digital-to-analog conversion. Also DAC.

D/A converter - This device converts digital information to analog form.

Daisy chain - A way of connecting a series of devices to a computer or to MIDI equipment. Device A is connected directly to the computer, device B to device A, device C to device B, etc.

Damping - Acoustical, electrical, or mechanical opposition to a moving system, as in a speaker voice coil assembly.

DAT - Digital Audio Tape (Recorder). *See* **R-DAT** and **S-DAT**.

Data - The information that the computer manipulates is called data. Data can be just about anything that can be expressed as patterns or numbers.

Data base - The data that the computer uses for a manipulation is called the data base.

Data base system - A program used to enter and display the information contained in a data base.

Data bytes - The bytes sent after a MIDI status byte to define the specific values of information being sent.

Data entry slider - A slide pot (potentiometer) that chooses data values.

Data file - A component of the data base; a block of data.

Data format - The way data in a data file is organized.

Data processor - A device that modifies data.

dB - *See* **Decibel.**

dBM - A decibel level in which one milliwatt of power dissipated in a 600 ohm line must also be measured in a 600 ohm line.

dBV - A decibel voltage level, in which the reference Vb, is 1.0 volt. A reference of 0.775 volts is also frequently used.

DB-25 - The male connector (DB-25M) and the female connector (DB-25S) are standard connectors used for cabling between RS-232 and compatible ports.

Dbx - The trademark of a noise reduction system used with multitrack tape machines.

DC - Direct Current. A constant signal of 0 Hz.

DCA - Digitally Controlled Amplifier. A device that controls the amplitude of a signal according to digital data.

DCC - Device Cluster Controller. *See* **Clustered devices.**

DC coupling - A method of transferring signals from one circuit to another that preserves frequencies down to 0Hz.

DCO - Digitally Controlled Oscillator. Used principally on Korg and Roland synthesizers, digital oscillators which can be directly controlled digitally.

DC offset - A small DC voltage at the output of an electronic stage.

DCW - Digitally Controlled Waveform. Casio's digital equivalent of an analog filter.

DDL - *See* **Digital delay line.**

Dead band - An area at the center of travel of a controller, e.g., a pitch-bend wheel within which movement of the controller has no effect.

Debounce - To prevent spurious closures of a key or switch from being recognized. *See* **Bounce.**

Debug - The process of locating and removing mistakes or malfunctions in a computer, piece of hardware or software.

Decay - *See* **Envelope.** The dying away of a note. In synthesizers, parts of the ADSR. In electronic music, decay refers to the amplitude characteristics at the end of a sound.

DeciBel (dB) - The unit of sound measurement. 0 dB is taken to be the threshold of hearing, while 130 dB is the threshold of pain. A normal speaking voice is about 65-70 dB.

Decoder - A device used to convert the coded digital-word pulse stream into an analog signal. A D/A converter.

Decrement - To decrease, usually by one.

Dedicated - Refers to a piece of equipment assigned to one particular use only, e.g., microprocessors.

Default - Some programs or systems allow you a choice of several options. If you do not pick one, one is automatically assigned by default.

DEG - Digital Envelope Generator. Korg's digital equivalent of an envelope.

Delay - To slow down the arrival of a signal by electronic means. Also, the time interval between a direct signal and its echo(es). *See* **Analog delay and digital delay line.**

Delayed vibrato - Vibrato added to a signal after the attack.

Delay line, digital - A delay line, in which the delay is accomplished electronically, via an analog/digital or digital/analog conversion.

Depth - The extent to which one parameter modulates another.

Desk - *See* **Console.**

Desk accessory - One computer program which can be called up while running another.

Detent - The center spot in a control's rotation, e.g., a synthesizer pitch bend wheel.

Detune - A control found on instruments that have two or more oscillators per voice, which is used to make changes in the pitch of one oscillator within a voice relative to the pitch of another.

Development software - Various computer programs which are specifically designed to facilitate the writing of other programs.

Diagnostic software - Software designed to determine if a computer is functioning properly and, if not, to determine what the problem is.

Dialog box - A box which shows on the computer screen that indicates the names of files extant, allows for the addition or deletion of files, or alerts the operator to a condition or malfunction.

Dielectric - In capacitors, an insulating layer between two conductors capable of maintaining an electric field.

Differential amplifier - An amplifier which produces a signal proportional to the difference between the signals of its two inputs.

Digital - Of the two main ways of doing things electronically, the digital method is to consider a circuit either on or off, a signal as either present or absent, with no levels in between. Digital equipment uses microprocessors to store and retrieve information about sound in the form of numbers and divides potentially continuous fluctuations in value into discrete quantized steps.

Digital/analog converter (DAC) - A device that will generate an analog voltage corresponding to the digital signal applied to it.

Digital/analog hybrid - *See* **Analog/digital hybrid.**

Digital delay line (DDL) - Similar to analog delay except that the effect is achieved by means of digital circuitry. *See* **Delay line, digital.**

Digitally controlled amplifier - *See* **DCA.**

Digitally controlled oscillator - *See* **DCO.**

Digitally controlled wave - *See* **DCW.**

Digital oscillator - An oscillator in which the specific waveshape to be generated exists in the form of a series of numbers that describe the height of the waveshape at various points in time.

Digital recording - A technique in which an analog signal is converted into a digital-format signal prior to recording. On playback, the digital data is converted back to the analog format.

Digital reverb - A device which processes an audio signal that simulates the effect of playing that signal in a particular space.

Digital sequencer - A sequencer in which the signals to be played back are stored as numbers in a digital memory.

Digital signal - A signal consisting of simple magnetic pulses used to represent numbers, symbols or other information that that can be expressed in digits.

Digital signal processing - After a sound or image has been digital-ized, it can be processed just like any other stream of numbers. Various interesting treatments are possible, such as the removal of noise, or the enhancement of contrast or detail. *See* **DSP**.

Digital system - In a computer system, the representation of all quanti-ties of information as a sequence of ON or OFF electrical pulses or bit patterns. A digital music system is one that employs a computer to store information related to the content or control of a piece of music. This digital information can then be converted to analog signals to generate sounds or control the generation of sounds using an analog voltage-controlled synthesizer.

Digital tape - Magnetic tape used to store information conveyed in a numerical sequence of impulses.

Digital-to-analog conversion - The conversion of digital information stored in a computer system to analog signals. These analog signals may be used to create music directly through a loudspeaker system or to provide control voltages to activate the sound-generating compo-nents of an analog synthesizer.

Digital-to-analog converter (DAC) - A device which converts (decodes) into a digital-format signal prior to recording. On playback, the digital data is converted back to the analog format.

Digit, binary - Any one of the two digits, 0 or 1, used in the binary numbering system.

Digitizer - A device that derives digital data from a nondigital source. *See* **Digitizing pad.**

Digitizing pad - Paper to accommodate a special pen which produces digital data that are input to a computer.

DIN - Deutche Industrie-Norm. Developed in Germany, a standard type of electrical connector.

DIN connector - Introduced in Europe, a type of multi-pin connector.

DIN sync - Clock-based synchronization method that serves as a system's common rhythmic reference.

Diode - An electronic component which converts AC into DC.

DIP - Dual Inline Package. The form in which most integrated circuits are made. Its two parallel rows of pins make it look not unlike a caterpillar.

Dip switch - An array of tiny switches packaged in the same manner as an integrate circuit, used to select options deep within some piece of hardware where they will not have to be changed frequently.

Direct connect modem - A modem connected directly to the telephone line, rather than through an acoustic coupler.

Direct coupling - Direct coupling avoids the use of capacitors for passing signals, in audio circuitry.

Direct current - *See* **DC**.

Direct memory access - *See* **DMA.**

Directory - A unit on a disk that contains files and possibly subdirectories. *See* **Catalog.**

Direct synthesis - A series of numbers representing the instantaneous values of voltage levels at different points in a waveform are stored in a computer memory, and called forth as necessary to produce the desired sound. The first experiments in direct synthesis were done at the Bell Telephone Laboratories, Murray Hill, New Jersey by Max Mathews in 1957.

Disabled - A device which has been given a signal that prevents it from functioning is said to be disabled.

Disk - A storage medium consisting of a magnetic surface on which data is stored, similar to the way sounds are recorded on tape. *See* **Floppy disk.**

Disk drive - A hardware component that stores and retrieves information on a disk. It can be a fixed disk drive or a floppy disk drive.

Diskette - Smaller disks, e.g., 3.5 and 5.25 inch types.

Display - A visual presentation of information on the screen.

Distortion - An unwanted change in waveform as it passes through an electronic component, or, from one medium to another.

Dither noise - Purposely injected noise used to ensure optimum operaion of a circuit's D-to-A converter.

DMA - Direct Memory Access. A way of speeding the process if the CPU temporarily surrenders control of memory to the peripheral.

Dolby system - Invented by Dr. Ray Dolby, a widely used tape noise reduction system which raises the high frequencies above normal. On playback, these are reduced to normal, greatly reducing the hiss.

Doppler effect - The frequency change of a sound wave caused by a continuous decreasing or increasing of the distance between the source and the listener.

DOS - Disk Operating System. A program that manipulates information on a disk, a DOS will allow you to write, erase, display, print files, and do many other things.

Dot matrix - A type of display that forms characters or images from many small points that are either on or off, present or absent. Versatile, but lacking in resolution unless a large number of points are used.

Dot-matrix printer - A printer that works by driving needles against the ribbon and paper. Although not as professional as a letter-quality printer, dot-matrix printers are usually quicker and less expensive.

Double density disk - *See* **Floppy disk.**

Double-ended noise reduction - *See* **Single-ended noise reduction.**

Double mode - *See* **Layering.**

Double sided disk- *See* **Floppy disk.**

Doubling - Mixing a slightly delayed signal with a direct signal, to simulate the effect of twice as many recorded instruments. Also, a deficiency of some speaker systems, in which low frequencies may be reproduced up one octave.

Downward-compatible - Devices that can run software from dated and less-apt products.

DPC - Data Processing Center.

Drag - In a computer, to move a mouse while holding one of its switches down.

DRAM - Dynamic Random Access Memory. *See* **Dynamic RAM.**

Drift - A change in the properties of an electrical circuit, as a result of temperature changes or aging. In a tape recorder, a long term deviation from the specified tape speed.

Driver - Software that provides for communication between a MIDI interface, a printer, etc., and a computer.

Droop - An unwanted variation in a control voltage, e.g., in earlier instruments, the keyboard voltage memory, which remembered what note had been played last, was prone to leakage, and the voltage would tend to decrease slowly.

Drop-down menus - Describes the action on a computer screen when the title bar "drops down" the menu options for selection.

Drum booth - An isolation booth, acoustically sealed off from the main recording studio, to enclose drummers, percussion instruments, etc., from players of other instruments.

Drum computer - A device which combines sampled drum sounds and sequencing to allow for the programming of drum patterns.

Drum machine - A device that reproduces the basic sounds of the drum set and fulfills the drummer's role as timekeeper, using computer-chip circuitry and programmable patterns.

Drum pad controllers - Drum pads that output MIDI information or trigger pulses when struck.

Drumslave - A MIDI circuit that converts trigger pulses generated by drum pads into MIDI data.

DSP - Digital Signal Processing. The process whereby analog signals are converted into digital data, data is manipulated, thus producing an analog output reflecting these changes.

DTR - Data Terminal Ready.

Dual inline package - *See* **DIP.**

Ducking - Lowering the level of an audio signal in response to another audio signal.

Dumb - Computer equipment which has no microprocessor-related circuitry nor software.

Dummy status byte - The status byte used in active sensing.

Dump - The act of transferring a large amount of data from one device to another; also, a trouble-shooting technique.

Duophonic - Two voices, one sounding the lowest note depressed on the keyboard and the other the highest. The simplified polyphonic synthesizer in which the two voices shared a single VCF and VCA was the duophonic synthesizer.

Duration - The length of time that a sound can be heard. The total duration of a sound relates to the attack, sustain, and decay characteristics of a sound. *See* **Envelope.**

Duty cycle - The percentage of a complete cycle of a pulse wave that it spends in the up portion of its cycle. Also called a pulse width.

DV-I - Digital Video Interactive. Originated by General Electric, a form of interactive video which is competitive with CD-I.

Dynamic - Refers to a process occuring during program execution.

Dynamic allocation - A way of assigning notes to voices in a multi-timbral synthesizer. This allows each timbre to be able to play as many voices as needed to perform a specific section.

Dynamic microphone - A moving coil or ribbon microphone. *See* **Microphone, dynamic.**

Dynamic RAM - A system of restoring memory which is occasionally lost by the computer.

Dynamic range - In a music instrument, a measure of the span between the quietest and loudest sounds it is capable of producing. In a tape recorder, the dB interval between the noise level and the level at which 3% distortion occurs. In a synthesizer, the term applies to the range of control that a touch responsive keyboard will provide.

Dynamics - The changes that take place over the duration of a sound. These changes are generally with respect to timbre and amplitude.

Ee

EAM - Electrical Accounting Machine.- An early term for computers.

EAROM - Electronically Alterable Read Only Memory. Unlike other types of ROM, it can be reprogrammed while still in the computer.

Echo - When data are being transmitted, the receiving device often re-transmits or "echoes back" the informaton so that the originating device can be sure it was received correctly. Also, the effect commonly achieved through the use of tape recorders with separate record and playback heads. *See* **Delay, DDL, Analog delay, Digital delay, Tape echo.**

Echo chamber - A live room containing speakers and microphones used to simulate natural reverberation.

Echoplex - A tape device which uses a tape loop and five recording heads to create echo effects. The recording heads are movable to enable echoes to be produced with any desired delay. In computers, a form of low-speed data transmission sometimes used between a keyboard device and a computer.

ECL - Emitter-coupled logic.

Edit - To change or modify information. Also, to change certain parameters of a sound, or to change part of a sequence.

Edit buffer - A temporary storing placing for data so it may be edited without disturbing the original data.

Edit mode - A mode of operation of a programmable synthesizer in which front-panel controls can be used to make temporary changes in the values stored in memory.

Educational Television (ETV) - A television system identified with open-channel, nonprofit community broadcasting stations.

EEPROM - Electronically Erasable Programmable Read Only Memory. A memory device that will store information even when the power is turned off. *See* **EAROM.**

Effects - Devices that change the characteristics of an audio signal passing through them, e.g., chorus, delay, equalization, flanging, panning, and reverb units.

Effects loop - In a guitar amp, pedal board or other equipment, connections which allow for insertion of an external signal processor into the audio chain.

Efx - Abbreviation for effects.

EG - *See* **Envelope generator.**

Eight(8)-bit -A term used to refer to digital audio systems in which sound data is manipulated and stored in the form of eight-bit words. *See* **Sixteen(16)-bit.**

Electret microphone - *See* **Microphone, electret.**

Electric bass - A bass instrument resembling a large guitar but is a four-stringed electric instrument which performs in the same register as an acoustic, or double bass. It was invented by Leo Fender in 1951 and originally sold as the Fender Precision Bass.

Electric guitar - Electric guitars were first designed by Lloyd Loar at the Gibson Company and manufactured by Loar and Lewis A. Williams at the Acousti-Lectric Company in 1934. Electric guitars, which are solid-bodied or hollow-bodied/semi-acoustic, usually have six strings tuned E-A-d-g-b-e1.

Electric organ - A term used to distinguish organs that include electro-acoustic or electro-mechanical elements from instruments in which the sound-generating system consists of electronic ocscillators.

Electric piano - First developed by Benjamin F. Miessner in 1932 in Milburn, New Jersey, the electric piano relied upon electroacoustic methods of sound production and included an amplifier and loudspeaker. Other early models used electrostatic pickups for the amplification system.

Electro-acoustics - The science of combining electrical and acoustical processes and devices which results in items such as microphones and loudspeakers.

Electroacoustic instruments - Acoustic instruments played in microphones, with contact pick-ups attached to them, or with built-in pickups.

Electrolytic capacitor - A capacitor which contains an electrolyte, a substance which produces an ionically conductive solution.

Electronic drums - *See* **Electronic percussion**.

Electronic instruments - Instruments in which the tone is produced, modified, or amplified by electronic circuits.

Electronic music - Music that is wholly or partially the result of the electronic generation, processing and reproduction of sound.

Electronic music instruments - Any music instrument whose sound is wholly or partially produced by electronic means.

Electronic music studio - A place where electronic music is created and usually contains tape recorders, sound modifiers, sound sources, envelope generators, amplifiers, etc.

Electronic percussion - Electronic instruments that synthesize percussion sounds or store and reproduce the sounds of acoustic percussion instruments, e.g., electronic drums, drum machines, rhythm machines, etc. The first electronic percussion instrument was the Rhythmicon designed by Lev Termen in 1931.

Electronic piano - Pianos in which the sound-generating system consists of electronic oscillators. The first electronic piano was developed in 1931 in Milburn, New Jersey by Benjamin F. Miessner and E.T. Jacobs.

Electrosonics - The science of producing sounds electronically, which includes noise, sonic experiments, music, etc.

Emphasis - *See* **Resonance.**

Emulation - The programming of one computer to imitate another computer.

Emulator board - A computer plug-in board that allows it to run programs originally written for a different computer.

Enabled - A device which has been given a signal that permits it to function is said to be enabled.

Encoder - A device which converts a quantized analog level into an encoded digital word. An A/D converter.

Endsteps - The physical limit of a control.

End user - The utilizer as opposed to the creator/marketer.

Engineer - A studio technician who establishes a recording environment, selects and operates the recording equipment, makes the final mix, and prepares the tape for mastering or other reproduction.

Envelope (ENV) - The attack, sustain, and decay characteristics of a sound. This is a function of amplitude related to the way a sound begins, continues, and ends. Attack is the time it takes for a sound to reach maximum loudness. Decay refers to the time it takes for a sound to end after having reached maximum loudness. Electronic musical devices offer voltage control over the envelope characteristics of sounds. Also, the overall shape of the waveform of a music instrument.

Envelope follower - An electronic device that generates a voltage reflecting the rise time, steady state, and decay characteristics of a signal applied to it. *See* **Envelope, Envelope generator.**

Envelope generator - The component of a synthesizer that sets DC control voltages to regulate the attack, sustain, and decay characteristics of sounds (voltages) produced through oscillators, filters, and amplifiers. *See* **ADSR.**

Envelope tracking - A function that changes the shape of the envelope depending on which key on a keyboard is being played. It is most often used to give higher notes on the keyboard proportionately shorter envelopes and lower notes longer envelopes, simulating acoustic systems.

EOF - End Of File. The final entry on a print-out.

EPROM - Erasable Programmable Read-Only Memory. Chips which can store information, be erased by exposure to UV light, and re-programmed, usually have EPROM.

Equalization (EQ) - The adjustment of the frequency response of an audio signal to obtain a desirable sound.

Equalizer - An electronic device for cutting or boosting selected frequencies. A sophisticated tone control.

Equalizer, graphic - An equalizer with a series of slide controls, arranged so as to give a graphic representation of the resulting frequency response.

Equalizer, parametric - An equalizer in which the frequency selector control is continuously variable over a wide range.

Equal temperament - A scaling system whereby the octave is divided into twelve equal parts. The frequency ratio between any two adjacent notes is exactly the same.

Erase - To remove data from a storage medium.

Error log - Imperfections in a hard disk which are noted to prevent data from being stored in these locations.

Error message - Each program should check for user mistakes and print error messages when they appear so that the user will know what is wrong.

ESCAPE (ESC) - In computers, an ASCII nongraphic character with the decimal value of 27 used to signify the start of a series of control characters.

Event - A distinct musical occurrence, with pitch, timbre, loudness and duration all defined.

Event-recorder - Used by some music-computer companies to describe a sequencer-type program. Notes, rests, and ties are all events in music and when a sequencer is described as an event recorder it usually means that the system will store information about which notes were played but will not store information about how they were played, key velocity, etc.

Expander - An electronic device for increasing the range of dynamics of an audio signal.

Expander module - A sound-generating module that responds to incoming MIDI data and generates sound.

Expert system - A program that systematizes the knowledge and rules of thumb used by an expert to arrive at decisions in his specialty.

Exponential - Opposite of linear, a relationship between two quantities such that a change in the amount of one is associated with a change in ratio of the other.

External sync - The mode on a drum machine or sequencer in which the device uses incoming MIDI timing clocks to determine its start, tempo, and stop.

Ff

Facsimile (FAX) - A technology for scanning photographs and visual documents, reducing images to digital form, transmitting them via a communications facilty, and reconstructing identical images at the receiving end.

Fader - The volume control on a mixing console, which is usually a sliding control rather than a knob.

FAX - *See* **Facsimile.**

FC - Center frequency, cutoff frequency. The fc is the center frequency of the resonant peak, in the case of a resonant filter.

Feedback - In amplified music, the reaction of the system - usually in the form of a sustained whining sound - when a portion of the output is fed back to the input. This can happen when a microphone is placed near a speaker so that it picks up the amplification of the sound it is feeding into the system. Multiple echoes are produced in a digital delay line using feedback. Also, a term often used to explain the resonance control of the filter, where some of the output is fed back to the input to accentuate the frequencies around the cutoff point.

FET - Field-Effect Transistor. A transistor which has an extremely high input impedance.

Fiber optics - A technology for transmitting information via light waves.

Fiche - High-resolution photographic material which can be written upon by a laser.

Fidelity - The measure of the degree of exactness with which sound is duplicated or reproduced.

Field-effect transistor. *See* **FET.**

File - A collection of related information with an identifying name. Programs and commands are contained in files, as are documents created with a word processor and organized data collections, such as spread-sheets and databases.

File format - The way in which file data is structured.

File name - The name assigned to a file when it is stored to disk. It is later used to recall the data into the computer.

Filter - An electronic processing device that can selectively pass certain frequency bands of a sound. *See* **Band-pass filter, Band-reject filter, High-pass filter**, and **Low-pass filter**. Synthesizer filters are generally capable of emphasizing certain frequencies in the region of the cutoff frequency, creating a resonant peak.

Filter, band pass - A filter that attenuates above and below a desired bandwidth.

Filter, band reject - A filter that attenuates a desired bandwidth, while passing frequencies above and below that bandwidth.

Filter, high pass - A filter that passes high frequencies, while attenuating those below a specified frequency.

Final mix, final mixdown - In recording, the final blending together of all the elements that have been taped during a recording session, resulting in the finished master tape.

Finder -The operating system that identifies disks, opens application software, copys and ejects, etc., in a Macintosh computer.

Fine-tune - A control that is used for making small, precise changes in the pitch of an oscillator.

Firmware - Software programmed into ROMS which cannot be changed.

5 pin DIN - The standard cable connectors used in MIDI.

Flam - A closely-spaced, double-attack of the same instrument electronically simulating a drum effect.

Flanging - A similar effect to phasing except that a wider variation in tape speed is used, giving the effect of a slight pitch deviation. *See* **Phasing.**

Floppy disk - A magnetic-coated plastic disk in a square protective cover, either 8", 5 1/4", or 3 1/2" in diameter, used for storing programs and files. *See* **Sector and track.**

Floppy-disk drive - A drive that reads and writes on a floppy disk, thereby passing information to and from a disk and the computer's memory.

FM - *See* **Frequency modulation.**

FM radio - FM operates at higher frequency bands than AM radio.

FM Synthesis - Frequency Modulation Synthesis. A method of creating sounds by means of the controlled frequency modulation of sine waves. Yamaha's patented sound-generation technique.

Footage - A way of designating which octave an oscillator will sound when a given note on the keyboard is played.

Footprint - The amount of space used by an electronic device.

Force sensitivity. *See* **Pressure sensitivity**.

Formant - A specific resonant frequency present in the harmonic spectrum of a music instrument which influences the tone color or timbre of the sound. Also, a resonant peak in a frequency spectrum.

Format - To prepare a disk to receive and store information by dividing the tracks on the surface of the disk into sectors in a manner compatible with MS-DOS. Formatting erases any previous data stored on the disk. Also, the method in which data is organized.

Format music - Music for syndicated advertising (jingles) that complies with any standard spot format.

FORTRAN - FORmula TRANslator. The most widely known computer language characterized by its simplicity and its expressions which have a strong resemblance to ordinary algebra.

Fourier analysis - The determination of the amplitude and frequency of each of the component sine waves in a complex waveform.

Fourier synthesis - The Fourier mathematical formula argues that any complex waveform may be resolved into a fundamental plus a set number of harmonics. This formula is widely used to allow computers to compute the gaps between information supplied about harmonic envelopes.

Four-pole - *See* **Rolloff slope.**

Free resonance - The natural phenomenon that causes the vibrations of one body to set off vibrations in a second body when the two bodies respond to identical frequencies.

Free-standing - Not part of a greater item of equipment.

Free time - The recording of a performance in actual time as opposed to electronically time-corrected to the nearest beat.

Frequency - The pitch of a sound, determined by the number of vibrations produced per second by the sounding body, measured in hertz.

Frequency modulation (FM) - In electronic music, the controlling of a signal (such as an oscillator) in order to alter the frequency or pitch of another signal. A variance in the pitch of the control signal will vary the pitch of the output signal in a corresponding amount.

Frequency offset - The difference in frequency between two oscillators.

Frequency range - The range between the highest and lowest pitched sounds which a tape recorder or other sound system component can reproduce at a usable output or volume level.

Frequency response - A graph of amplitude vs. frequency.

Frequency spectrum - The audible frequency range of human hearing, which is approximately 20 Hz to 20,000 Hz (Hz being a designation for the number of vibrations per second).

FSK - Frequency Shift Keying. A type of synchronization signal that consists of a rapid periodic alternation between two pitched audio tones, usually an octave or more apart. FSK is often used to synchronize drum machines and sequencers to tape.

Function - A special subroutine kept in the computer's memory which may include square root, log, absolute value, and trig functions.

Function keys - The F1 through F10 keys on the left side of the keyboard of some computers. When pressed, they perform certain editing operations on the MS-DOS command line. Function keys are often programmable and have different meanings according to what program is being run.

Function parameters - Parameters that relate to live performance setups, e.g., breath controller modulation, pedal functions, pitch bend range, etc., in Yamaha equipment.

Fundamental - The primary note of a chord. In music acoustics, the lowest frequency component of a sound, to which are added higher partials or overtones. The fundamental is sometimes called the first harmonic. In waveshaping, the root harmonic on which other harmonics are built. Also, in analysing a waveshape, the fundamental is the lowest frequency element present.

Fundamental frequency - The common divisor of all harmonics of a waveform. Also, the frequency of a waveform where the greatest concentration of energy occurs.

Fuzz bass - A loud and sustained sound produced by an amplified electric bass channeled through a distortion booster.

Fuzz box - A device which breaks up the sound passing through it, causing a distorted sound simulating that of a valve amplifier being over driven.

FX - Abbreviation for effects.

Gg

Gain - The amount of increase or decrease of volume.

Gate - A digital circuit which produces an output only for certain conditions of input. Also, a control signal put out by a keyboard that tells the envelope generators that a key is now depressed, or an equivalent signal put out by a manual switch, sequencer, or some other module. In a movie camera, the part that has an opening to allow light from the lens to expose the film.

GEM - Graphics Environment Manager. Developed by Digital Research, the name of the user interface that's part of Atari's ST computer operating system, TOS.

Generation - A copy of a tape, i.e., the original recording is a first generation tape; a copy, a second generation, etc.

GFI - *See* **Ground fault interrupter.**

Glide - A portamento, in which the pitch slides smoothly from one note to the next instead of jumping over the intervening part of the frequency spectrum. *See* **Auto-bend, auto-glide.**

Glissando - A continuous gliding through pitches either up or down the scale.

Glitch - A bit of electrical noise that causes circuits to misbehave. By extension, the term refers to any minor but irritating foul-up.

Global operations - Operatons which affect an entire system as opposed to a subset of the system.

Go down - Letting the system "go down". Turn the machine off.

Graphic editing - Instead of using text or numbers, editing that displays and uses data pictorially.

Graphic equalizer - An equalizer using small linear faders which permits manual control over a wide range of selectable frequencies. *See* **Equalizer, graphic.**

Graphic interface - The use of graphic symbols called icons as a way of communicating with a computer.

Graphics display - A CRT screen built specifically for displaying graphics.

Ground - A point in an electrical circuit used as the zero voltage reference and which is connected to the earth or a part of the circuit serving as the earth.

Ground fault interrupter - A safety device which interrupts AC current flow when a ground is defective.

Ground loop - The path in a ground circuit between two or more points intended to be at the same voltage but which are not because of ground resistance.

Growl - Low frequency sine wave modulation of the filter cut-off frequency.

Guitar controller - A device that outputs MIDI data, which plays like a guitar, instead of or in addition to a regular guitar sound.

Guitar synthesizer - A synthesizer designed to work with a guitar controller which is operated with foot controls.

Hh

Haas effect - Also called precedence effect, human audio ability to ascertain the direction from which sound emanates.

Half-height drive - A disk drive that uses only half the standard height for a type of drive.

Hamograph - An electronic control device for use in the creation of electronic music. It coordinates timbre, rhythm, pitch and spatial effects with the help of independent multiple loudspeaker units in as many as six separate voices.

Hand shaking - The continual exchange of transmissions from one machine to another.

Hard copy - Information in a form that you can carry away with you and examine at your leisure.

Hard disk - A mass storage device based on an aluminum disk or platter coated with magnetic oxide in which the read/write head does not touch the disk (as it does with a floppy disk), but rides on a thin cushion of air.

Hard disk drive - A computer disk drive that uses a metal disk instead of a floppy disk.

Hard disk recording - Hard disks are used in a recording system since digitized audio signals take up a large amount of memory.

Hard hit - A percussive musical accent that highlights an on-screen event in film and video scoring.

Hard sync - The standard type of oscillator sync. *See* **Sync.**

Hardware - The physical parts of the computer; e.g., system unit, disk drives, printer, etc.

Hardware configuration - The various devices that constitute a computer system, e.g., disks, printers, tape drives, etc.

Hard-wired - Connected permanently. The opposite of patchable.

Harmonic - Overtones whose frequencies are usually some multiple of the frequency of the fundamental.

Harmonic analyzer - An electronic device used to calculate the relative strength of all the partials present in a complex waveform.

Harmonic distortion - The intended or unintended introduction of additional overtones during the electronic processing of a signal.

Harmonics - Numerous frequencies are present in a pitched tone. The fundamental frequency is either the lowest or the loudest frequency present in the note. Additional frequencies above the fundamental are called overtones or harmonics.

Harmonic series - A composite of the many harmonics that vibrate along with the fundamental in a complex tone.

Harmonic theory - The characteristic tone quality of an instrument is due to the relationship among fundamental and upper partials, in which the relationship is supposed to remain unchanged no matter what the fundamental. *See* **Harmonic series.**

Harmonizer - A device which electronically changes the pitch of a signal without affecting tempo; trademarked by the Evintide Corporation.

HDTV - High-Density Television. Compared to standard television systems in the U.S., a system that produces much-improved picture resolution.

Head - A small electromagnet used to read or write information onto the magnetic surface of a tape, disk, or drum. On a tape recorder, the transducer used to apply and/or detect magnetic energy on the tape.

Headroom - The gap between the peak working level on tape and the point at which the sound might actually distort. In computers, having sufficient spare computing power. In magnetic recording tape, the dB difference between standard operating level (+4dBm) and the 3% distortion point.

Hertz (Hz) - Designation for the number of cycles per second of a periodic frequency, which is named for Heinrich Hertz.

Heterodyne - The process whereby two signals of different frequencies are combined in order to produce two other frequencies equal to the sum and difference of the original frequencies.

Heterodyning - In electronic music, a method for mixing multiple signals of near-equal frequencies that results in a cancellation of the given tones and the creation of beat frequencies or wavering (tremolo) effects. The sound-generating method used in the Theremin. A form of amplitude modulation.

Hexadecimal - A number system which uses 16 digits. Hexadecimal (hex) is a very compact way of representing binary numbers and especially convenient when the word length is a multiple of four. The following is a counting example to 16 in decimal, hexadecimal, and binary:

Decimal	Hexadecimal	Binary
0	0	0000
1	1	0001
2	2	0010
3	3	0011
4	4	0100
5	5	0101
6	6	0110
7	7	0111
8	8	1000
9	9	1001
10	A	1010
11	B	1011
12	C	1100
13	D	1101
14	E	1110
15	F	1111
16	10	10000

Hex pickup - A guitar pickup that has an individual audio output for each string.

Hierarchical structure - Also, a tree structure, a method of organizing data in a logical, orderly way, including a sorting process.

Hierarchy - The process/order used in a structure based on organizing data in a logical, orderly way.

High-density television - *See* **HDTV.**

High end - A term denoting sounds with a frequency higher than 5kHz.

High fidelity - Sound reproduction of high quality that strives to reproduce a live music sound.

High-level language - Languages such as BASIC, FORTRAN, ALGOL, COBOL, and PL/I are some widely used high-level languages. These allow for the programmer to write English-like instructions which the computer then translates into machine language.

Highlighted data - Emphasizing important data on a computer screen by brightening the picture, placing it in an enclosed box, shading it, etc.

High-note priority - A keyboard logic found on some monophonic synthesizers and some polyphonics whey they are in unison mode, in which the highest key depressed is the one whose control signal is sent to the oscillators.

High-pass filter - An electronic filter that only permits frequencies above a specified cutoff point to be heard. A common component of synthesizers. *See* **Filter, high pass.**

High-resolution graphics - Computer graphics that have more detail than low or medium graphics.

Hi-resolution - Auto-correction in small units resulting in the equivalent to playing in free time.

Histogram - A horizontal bar chart, printed on a computer printer, to graph statistical information.

Hit - A percussive music accent that highlights an on-screen event, in film and video scoring.

Hold - *See* **Latching**. Also, the MIDI code sent when a sustain pedal is pressed which commands instruments to continue holding notes that are being played after a MIDI note-off message has been received.

Holography - The construction of three-dimensional images using graphics software and display devices.

Hum - A low-pitched drone coming from electronic equipment. It usually derives from the main power supply.

Humanize - In order to gain a more natural sound, to add minute variations in computerized music.

Hybrid - In England, a design group based in Covent Garden.

Hybrid synthesis - An alternative method to direct synthesis in which some or all of the control circuits for a conventional synthesizer are connected to a network of digital-to-analog converters, allowing their performance characteristics to be regulated by a computer.

Hybrid synthesizer - A synthesizer that is a combination of analog sound generating elements with digital control.

Hydrophones - Transducers designed to pick up underwater sounds.

Hysteresis loop - A graph of magnetizing force vs. remanent magnetization.

Hz - Abbreviation for hertz, the unit measurement of frequency.

Ii

IBM AT - An IBM PC which uses an 80286 microprocessor, making it six to twelve times more powerful and efficient than the original PC, with 16 megabytes as opposed to 1 megabyte more memory.

IBM-compatible - Any hardware which is capable of using the same software as IBM PC.

Icon - Representing a command, data file, or program, a symbol displayed on a computer screen which is activated by the cursor or a mouse.

Icon-based interface - *See* **Graphic interface.**

IFF - *See* **Interchange File Format.**

Illegal commands - Instructions the computer is unable to recognize.

IM - *See* **Intermodulation distortion.**

IMA - International MIDI Association. An association which provides information about MIDI to end users, schools, technicians, and other interested parties.

Imitative synthesis - By using music synthesis techniques, a process of sonically simulating acoustic and electronic instruments.

Impedance - The opposition of a circuit to the flow of alternating current. Impedance is the complex sum of resistance and reactance.

Impressionistic synthesis - Using music synthesis techniques, a process of creating unprecedented sounds.

Impulse - A brief, sudden surge of current or voltage having no definite pitch or timbre.

IMUG - International MIDI Users Group, the original name of the IMA (International MIDI Association).

Increment - To increase.

Incrementer - An alpha dial, usually assigned to one of several parameters, which can be rotated to increase or decrease a value.

Inductance - An opposition to a change in current.

Inductor - An electronic component that opposes a change in current.

Infinite repeat - A function on reverbs and digital delays which may continuously repeat a stored signal.

Information system - Any coordinated combination of computer software, hardware, and data that work together for a specific set of goals.

Initialize - The start-up procedure for computer systems using peripheral units such as disk drives or printers. The initialization program sets up the starting condition.

Input - Information entered into a program, rather than information produced by a computer program. A signal received by a recorder, mixer or signal processor. Also, the point at which an audio signal enters a recorder, mixer or signal processor.

Input/output (I/O) - Connection point through which the computer receives and/or transmits data.

Input/output module - On an in-line console, a single module containing input, output and monitor controls for a single audio channel.

Install - Same as configure.

Institutional spot - A jingle designed to promote a company image in radio or television.

Instruction - A coded program step that tells the computer what to do next.

Instructional Television (ITV) A closed-circuitor broadcasting television system that only offers educational instruction.

Insulator - Any material that resists the flow of electricity.

Integrated circuit (IC) - A tiny chip of silicon several millimeters square that has been subjected to a series of diffusions and etchings resulting in the equivalent of several thousand interconnected transistors.

Intelligence - A machine's ability to operate and modify behaviour under the control of an internal program.

Intelligent - In computer programs, the ability to make decisions as well as manipulate data.

Interactive computing - An environment in which a person at a keyboard terminal and a computer conduct a dialog through entering data, editing, and executing programs.

Interchange file format (IFF) - A file format which allows for the transfer of images, sounds, and texts between programs and computers.

Interface - A device which connects two different instruments which allows for the transformation of signals, e.g., interfacing a sequencer and synthesizer.

Intermittent - Problems which occur unpredictably.

Intermodulation distortion - Signal distorion which is more troublesome than harmonic distortion.

Internal sync - The mode in which a drum machine or sequencer uses its own clock to determine tempo.

Interpreter - A program that causes the computer to scan each instruction, decide what it is being told to do, and then do it.

Interval - The pitch ratio between two tones.

Interval ambit - The number of different linear intervals used in a music work. Also, the amount of frequency difference between two pitches.

Interval control - A control which adjusts the pitch offset between two tone generators in a two-tone-generator-per-voice system.

Inverter - A device that changes positive voltages into negative voltages and vice versa, thus reversing the phase on periodic signals.

Inverting amplifier - Compared to the input, an amplifier whose output is 180 degrees out of phase.

I/O bound - When the computer's CPU spends most of its time waiting for input or output devices to finish instead of doing calculations.

I/O device - *See* **Input/output** device. The method of transferring data in and out of the computer to an external device such as a printer or disk drive.

IPS - Inches per second.

Isolation - The acoustic or electrical separation of one sound source from another.

Isolation booth - A small room, used to acoustically separate a soloist from the rest of a music group being recorded at the same time. *See* **Drum booth, vocal booth.**

Jj

Jack - A female socket used to receive a plug for connecting and continuing an electronic circuit. *See* **Patch chord, Patch panel,** etc.

Jack bay - In a recording console or equipment rack, a strip of female input and output sockets, used in conjunction with patch cords for signal routing purposes. Also, jack field, patch bay.

Jargon - Slang words used in fields of expertise, in general, and in the computer-electronic field, in particular.

JES - Job Entry System. The systems software that accepts and schedules jobs for execution and controls printing of output, in large-scale computer systems.

Jingle - Music written and/or recorded for use in a radio or television commercial.

Joystick - A controller for modulating sounds, mostly used on synthesizers in place of pitch and modulation wheels, but can also be used as a pan-pot for multiphonic sound systems.

Justification - The alignment of data within a field, in computers.

Just intonation - A scaling system whereby the octave is divided into twelve unequal divisions.

Kk

K - Abbreviation for 1,000.

K - *See* **Kilo, Kilobyte**.

Kbyte - *See* **Kilobyte**.

Key - In software, a piece of information associated with a record and used to identify it for purposes of sorting, retrieval, etc. In signal processing, changing the amount or type of processing a device performs on a program signal by using a separate control signal.

Keyboard - The hardware device with a panel of keys that is used to type data or execute commands. Also, a controller used primarily for playing traditional melodic and harmonic patterns. Also, a row of black and white keys used to play notes on a synthesizer.

Keyboard amount - *See* **Keyboard tracking.**

Keyboard code - *See* **Key code.**

Keyboard controller - A piano-type keyboard used to activate voltage controls to produce sounds in an electronic-music synthesizer.

Keyboard following - *See* **Envelope tracking.**

Keyboard logic - A system that determines what signals are sent out from the keyboard and where they are routed.

Keyboard priority - Various systems are employed to assign the voice module to the notes played on the keyboard. The priority modes sort out which note is to sound when more than one is activated on a monophonic instrument. *See* **Low, High, and Last note priority.**

Keyboard scaling - The smooth variation in amplitude of a sound or some component of a sound over the range of the keyboard. Also, the calibration of an oscillator so that moving from any key to an adjacent key produces the required pitch change.

Keyboard setup - Edit parameters that are separate from the voice patch but affect it, and can be stored separately or alongside the patch, e.g., pitch-bend range, split point, transpose, etc.

Keyboard splits - A music keyboard feature that enables different patches to be played at the same time on different sections of the keyboard.

Keyboard tracking - Controlling some element of the sound, usually the cutoff frequency of the filter, with a voltage or equivalent pitch information from the keyboard.

Key disk - A device which allows the owner of an original key disk to make copies.

Key number - A numerical value for each key of a keyboard, e.g., MIDI has 128 key numbers.

Keypad - The cluster of special-purpose keys on the terminal keyboard to one side of the regular typing keys, on some machines.

Keys-down - Information from musical-keyboard keys: how hard the key was played, how fast it was pushed down, how long it was held down, etc. This is the keys-down information that a high-quality music computer system should be able to read from the keyboard.

Keystroke - One press of a key on an alphanumeric keyboard.

Key velocity - *See* **Velocity.**

kHz - Kilohertz. A unit of frequency equal to 1,000 cycles per second or hertz.

Kilo - A prefix, k, for thousand. 10 kohms = ten thousand ohms.

KiloBaud - A unit of data transfer equal to 1,000 bits per second.

Kilobyte (K) - 1,024 bytes.

KiloHertz (kHz) - Hertz measured in multiples of 1,000. 10 kHz = 10,000Hz.

KilOhm - 1,000 Ohms.

Kluge - A messy circuit or modification.

Ll

Ladder filter - *See* **Moog filter.**

Lag - An effect that smooths out rapid changes in voltage which is obtained by using a very low frequency low pass filter.

Lag processor - A device that smooths out sudden changes in voltage.

LAN - Local Area Network. A way of linking a number of computers through communication lines so that the computer can locate it.

Language - The set of rules, words and symbols used to write a program for a computer, e.g., BASIC, COBOL, FORTRAN, LISP, etc.

Laptop computer - A portable computer which can be manipulated on one's lap.

Large scale integrated circuit - *See* **LSI.**

Laser - In multimedia, an intense beam of directed light usually connected by its beam to a receiving device, usually in turn, leading to an oscillator which triggers the oscillator when the beam is broken.

Laser printer - A printer that uses laser technology. *See* **Dot-matrix printer** and **Letter-quality printer.**

Last-note priority - A keyboard logic in which each new key, as it is depressed, activates a voice taking over a voice that had previously been sounding the pitch of another key.

Latching - A simplified memory system in which the synthesizer continues to operate according to whatever latchable pattern was in effect at the moment the latching switch was cued in, until it is released. Also, a procedure that memorizes a certain parameter, e.g., the interval between two oscillators.

Layering - Overdubbing or recording one track at a time. Also, adding layers of sound, e.g., sounding two or more voices, each of which generally has its own timbre, from each key depression.

LCD - Liquid Crystal Diode. A device consisting of a special liquid sealed between two sheets of glass; a display system often found in inexpensive electronic items.

Least significant bit - *See* **LSB.**

LED - Light Emitting Diodes. LED's are incorporated into VU meters to reflect transient peaks of volume.

Leslie speaker - A system which includes separate rotating low and high frequency speakers. It was designed by Donald J. Leslie in 1940 and manufactured by the Electro-Music Company, Pasadena, California.

Letter quality printer - A printer that produces fully-formed characters like those of a typewriter and is suitable for correspondence.

LFO - Low-frequency oscillator. An oscillator devoted to sub-audio applications, and used as a control source for producing vibrato, tremolo, trills, etc.

Library - A collection of programs in each computer for doing routine tasks.

Light metronome - A metronome (device that beats time) that flashes a light on and off, silently, at a given tempo.

Light pen - A high-speed pen-shaped device which, when held against a CRT, can issue instructions for program or graphics purposes.

Limiter - A signal-processing device that reduces volume peaks without coloring the overall dynamic range. Generally, a compressor with a compression ratio of 10:1 or greater.

Linear - A straight line, without bends or kinks. Linear amplifiers produce no distortion. Also, a linear relationship between two values is such that a change in one causes a proportional change in the other. *See* **Exponential.**

Linear FM - Frequency modulation in which the center frequency of the carrier oscillator is not altered by a change in the amount of modulation.

Linear potentiometer - A pot (potentiometer) whose resistance changes at a constant linear rate. *See* **Audio taper potentiometer.**

Linear power supply - *See* **Switching power supply.**

Line conditioner - Less effective than a UPS (uninterruptible power system), a line conditioner compensates for surges and/or filters AC power negatively affected by voltage variations.

Line printer - A piece of equipment that prints out information on wide sheets of paper, a full line at a time.

Lip sync - When pre-recorded sound is used, the synchronization of picture and sound to give the effect of live oral performance.

Listening station - A unit designed for listening that contains a variety of sound sources, e.g., record players, tape recorders, etc.

Lithium battery - A long-life battery with low current drain.

Live-electronic music - Music in which certain aspects are created and modified by electronic equipment at the time of performance.

Load - To transfer data and programs from a disk into the computer's memory. To enter data. Also, a specified amount of power in an electronic device.

Local control - A feature in MIDI that indicates the source of control of a keyboard's voice generators.

Local/remote switch - A synthesizer switch that determines if tones will be generated from a remote keyboard by MIDI codes, or in response to its own keyboard.

Lock - To prevent a file from being changed or erased.

Lockout - A situation during computer operation when the arithmetic and logic units both try to access the CPU at the same time. The computer will cease to work.

Logarithm - That power to which 10 must be raised to equal a number, i.e., the logarithm of 1,000 is 3, since $10(3) = 1,000$.

Logarithmic potentiometer - *See* **Audio taper potentiometer.**

Logic family - Sympathetic electronic semiconductor-based components used to implement a digital hardware system.

Logic operation - Electronically manipulating two pieces of information according to the rules of logic, e.g., AND, NAND, NOR, OR, and XOR.

Loop - A sequence of computer instructions that is executed repeatedly until a specified condition is satisfied. Also, a closed path designed for the continuous flow of electrical current. Also, a piece of material that plays repetitively. *See* **Tape loop.**

Loudness - The subjective impression of the intensity of a sound.

Low frequency noise component - A non-periodic element of a signal.

Low frequency oscillator - *See* **LFO**.

Low-level language - A programming language that closely resembles the instructions that the processor executes when it runs a program. *See* **Assembly language.**

Low-note priority - A type of keyboard logic found on some mono-phonic synthesizers and on some polyphonics when they are in unison mode, in which the lowest key depressed is the one whose control signal is sent to the oscillators.

Low-pass filter - An electronic filter that permits only frequencies below a specified cutoff point to be heard. A common component of synthesizers.

LP - Long playing (33 1/3 rpm) phonograph record.

LPI - Lines Per Inch.

LSB - Least Significant Byte. Used for increasing the resolution of some MIDI controllers, a second data byte.

LSI - Large Scale Integrated Circuit. The technology which makes it possible to produce CPU'S and other complex circuits in a single integrated circuit.

LSTTL - A faster and more efficient version of the TTL logic group.

Mm

M - Meg or mega, 1M ohm = 1,000,000 ohms.

mA - Abbreviation for milliAmpere, i.e., 1/1,000th of an Ampere.

Machine language - Binary language, the language of 0 and 1 that functions on all computers. Instructions for the synthesis or composition of music by computer are usually set down in a specific program which is then translated into machine language.

Macro - In computers, a combination of commands that may be called by one computer command or keystroke.

Mainframe - The main part of the computer, the CPU. Also used to describe the large ultra-powerful computers operated by governments and multi-national corporations.

Main memory - In the computer, the memory that the processor can directly read information from or write to.

Main menu - In computers, the initial menu that appears when a program is loaded.

Mass storage - The section of the computer that stores large amounts of data, e.g., floppy or hard disks.

Master - Any device that controls the operation of other components. *See* **Slave**. Also, to cut a lacquer or direct metal master for a record or a CD master.

Master device - A device that controls several other slave devices, in MIDI.

Master keyboard- Designed to control other MIDI devices by means of MIDI messages, a music keyboard without built-in sound generators.

Master synth - The synthesizer that controls other synthesizers via MIDI code outputs.

Master volume - The last level-regulating element in a signal chain.

Matrixing - The three-step process in CD and record production by which metal parts are made.

Matrix panel - A patching system in which inputs and outputs for all modules are brought to a central grid and connected to one another using switches or pins.

Mb, mbyte or meg - One megabyte.

Meg - Megabyte.

Mega - A prefix meaning one million.

Megabytes (M) - Megabytes = 1,048,576 bytes = 1,024 kilobytes.

Megaflop - A rate of computer throughput equal to one million floating point arithmetical operations per second.

Megahertz - A frequency unit equal to one million cycles per second or one million hertz.

Megs - More than one megabyte.

Membrane switch - A very sensitive switch.

Memory - The area of the computer that temporarily stores programs and data while the computer is on. The computer can quickly access what is currently in memory. Most programs come on a floppy disk. Usually, when you run a program, a disk drive transfers the program, or parts of it, from the floppy disk to the computer's memory. A floppy disk is permanent storage and the computer's memory is temporary storage. Memory is measured in kilobytes. *See* **Byte**. Also, a buffer into which program segments may be transferred in order to be digitally manipulated. *See* **Storage**. Synthesizer memories are used for storing patches, sequences of notes, keyboard split points, etc.

Memory bank - A section of a computer in which coded information is stored.

Memory location - In computers, a single unit of memory that is identified by a unique address and can hold a piece of information.

Memory protection - When valuable information is lost when it is overwritten by a runaway program, memory can be put into a protect mode, so that it may be read from but not written into.

Memory resident - A program loaded into memory (RAM) rather than on disk.

Menu - A list of alternatives presented by a program for the user to choose among.

Menu bar - Also termed title bar, a moving bar which allows one to select a command or option from a menu.

Menu-driven - A software-design style in which the program offers the user a menu of choices whenever a decision has to be made.

Mercury battery - A constant output voltage battery.

Merge - To combine two files into one while keeping the original order. In MIDI, a device that allows two separate digital streams of MIDI data to be combined.

Merger - *See* **MIDI merger.**

Message - *See* **Error message or screen message.**

Message filler - A MIDI recorder feature that allows for the removal of certain types of messages from incoming or outgoing MIDI data.

Metal tape - A tape which delivers more high frequency headroom and requires higher bias than ferric or chrome tape.

MG - Modulation Generator. Refers to the LFO section of instruments of some manufacturers, e.g., Korg.

mHz - Abbreviation for megahertz.

Micro - Microprocessor. Also, one millionth.

Microamp - A unit of current measurement equal to 1/1,000,000th of an Ampere.

Microcomputer - A small computer system, usually based on one or two microprocessors.

Microelectronics - Electronic technology involved with semi-conductor chips using large-scale integration.

Microfloppy - A 3.5 inch floppy disk.

Microphone, condenser - The popular name for a capacitor microphone.

Microphone, dynamic - A moving coil or ribbon microphone.

Microphone, electret - A microphone with a permanently charged capacitor/diaphragm.

Microphone, preamplifier - In a recording console, the first stage of amplification, which raises microphone levels to line level. Also, the amplifier built into a condenser microphone.

Micropower mode - A memory circuit mode used in equipment with battery backup.

Microprocessor - The CPU (Central ProcessingUnit) of a computer built in layers on a microscopic chip of silicon. It is used in sophisticated digital outboard equipment and units such as sequencers and drum machines, and in automated or computer mixing consoles.

Microsecond - A millionth of a second.

Microwave - A high-frequency radio communications technology utilizing point-to-point beams aimed using dish antennas.

MIDI - Musical Instrument Digital Interface. A computer language that allows different types of music hardware, e.g., computers, drum machines, sequencers, synthesizers, etc., to communicate with each other.

MIDI adaptor - A device that adds MIDI ports to a computer.

MIDI cable - A cable with 5-pin plugs on each end to carry messages between MIDI devices.

MIDI channel - *See* **Channel.**

MIDI clog - When a MIDI device or several MIDI devices overburden MIDI cables with messages, "MIDI clog" results.

MIDI code - Digital data-transmission format by which MIDI-generating/receiving devices communicate with each other.

MIDI continuous controller - A computer control that replaces synthesizer parameters previously controlled by physical devices.

MIDI delay - When an excess of events is sent into the MIDI, MIDI delay is experienced.

MIDI device - A device which is equipped with MIDI ports and a microprocessor.

MIDI implementation - MIDI functions available in a piece of equipment.

MIDI implementation sheet - A one-page summary of a device's MIDI implementation.

MIDI In - A connector that receives MIDI data received from a MIDI Out connector on another unit.

MIDI interface - A device that adds MIDI ports to a computer.

MIDI lag - A delay in passing MIDI messages from the MIDI In port to a MIDI Thru port.

MIDI Manufacturers Association - MMA.

MIDI merger - A program or accessory device that receives data from two or more MIDI devices and combines it into one MIDI output.

MIDI message - Data sent between MIDI devices that communicates a single music idiom, e.g., the starting of a note or a bend in the pitch.

MIDI mode - *See* **Mode.**

MIDI patch bay - A device that reconfigures unit-to-unit patching of MIDI devices.

MIDI port - A 5-pin socket built into a MIDI device.

MIDI recorder - Computer software that records incoming MIDI messages, allows for editing, and plays back using attached MIDI devices.

MIDI sequencer - An electronic device that generates continuous MIDI code to trigger electronic devices, e.g., drum machines, synthesizers, etc.

MIDI sequencer, computer - A computer that utilizes a software program to emulate the operation of a MIDI sequencer.

MIDI/SMPTE synchronizer - A device which interprets SMPTE signals and MIDI messages and can use them to synchronize SMPTE and MIDI devices.

MIDI sync - The mode on a drum machine or sequencer that causes it to start, stop and play at the same tempo as a drum machine or sequencer connected to it.

MIDI switch controller - *See* **MIDI continuous controller.**

MIDI switcher - A device that reconfigures unit-to-unit MIDI patching.

MIDI-thru - A connector found on some MIDI equipment that provides a copy at the MIDI In connector.

MIDI-thru box - A circuit that divides a single MIDI signal into separate signals, each capable of driving a separate slave device.

MIDI-thru inputs/outputs - Some synthesizers have a MIDI input which extracts the channels of data needed to control that synthesizer from an incoming MIDI signal, regenerates and passes all other MIDI data to the output.

MIDI Time Code - MIDI messages which allow MIDI gear to trigger events by times related to SMPTE time code.

MIDI volume - Identified as Controller #7, a MIDI controller that affects the overall audio output level.

Mil - One thousandth of an inch.

Milli - One thousandth.

Milliamp - *See* **mA**.

Millisecond - One thousandth of a second.

Minicomputer - Early minicomputers had a word length of 18 bits or less, about 4K of memory, but have greatly improved in capacity and speed.

Mini-floppy - An original term for the 5.25 inch disk.

MIPS - Million Instructions Per Second. A crude indicator of performance for larger computers.

Mix - Abbreviation for mixdown.

Mixdown - *See* **Mixing**.

Mixer - An audio device for combining or mixing sound from multiple sources. *See* **Fader.** Also, the engineer who mixes or dubs the soundtracks of an audio and/or video-film recording.

Mixing - The process of balancing and adjusting existing tracks on a multitrack machine and transferring them on to two- or four-track tape.

MMA - MIDI Manufacturers Association.

Mode - The way in which a device is operating. In MIDI, omni-on poly, aka omnimode; omni-on mono; omni-off poly, aka poly mode; and, omni-off mono, aka mono mode.

Modem - MODulation/DEModulation. A device that converts computer output (which is digital) to an analog form. This makes it possible to send and receive information from a computer over a telephone line.

Modem eliminator - A device whose electronics simulate the appropriate control signals of a modem between two communicating machines.

Mode messages - The MIDI commands used to change the mode of an instrument.

Modem port - The section of a computer to which the modem connects.

Modifier - Any electronic device that changes a characteristic or characteristics of a signal. *See* **Amplifier, Reverberation unit, Modulator, Filter, etc.**

Modular - Composed of sub-units. Computer systems and programs are made this way to make them easier to change or expand. Also, a type of synthesizer design in which the various sound sources are semi-independent pieces of hardware that must be hooked together with patch chords or some other patching system.

Modular synthesizer - A synthesizer whose elements are available as independent units, e.g., controllers, sound generators, sound modifiers, etc.

Modulate - To vary the amplitude, frequency, phase, etc.

Modulation - The modification of an electronic sound source through the action of other electronic sources. Frequency modulation and amplitude modulation are two.

Modulation index - The ratio between the output level of a modulator operator and the level of the carrier it is modulating. An FM synthesis term.

Modulation pedal - Same as a modulation wheel except controlled by a foot device.

Modulation wheel - The controller on a synthesizer which is used for sending modulation, usually in the form of vibrato.

Modulator - An electronic instrument that produces a signal used to alter the characteristics of another signal. *See* **Modulation.**

Module - A unit of circuitry or individual instrument which can be added to or removed from an electronic equipment network.

Monaural - Sound reproduction involving only one channel as opposed to stereophonic sound which involves two or more channels.

Monitor - The computer screen. It can be either monochrome or color. Also, in recording, a loudspeaker used in studio control rooms to determine quality or balance. Stage monitors are used by performers so that they can hear themselves. Also, a computer system program that coordinates the rest of the system.

Monochord - An effect possible on a monophonic, multioscillator synthesizer in which the oscillators are tuned to certain intervals, and this fixed chord is transposesd by the keyboard's (controller) control voltage.

Monochrome - One color.

Mono mode - In MIDI, one of three operating modes. In mono, an instrument responds monophonically to all note information received over a specific MIDI channel.

Monophonic - Capable of playing only one note at a time. Such instruments are used primarily for playing melodies. Also, pertaining to an audio system in which the entire program is heard from a single sound source.

Monophonic synthesizer- A synthesizer that can play notes using only one patch at a time.

Moog - A synthesizer manufacturing company founded by Robert A. Moog in 1964 in Trumansburg, New York. Since 1973 Moog Music has been a division of Norlin Industries. Moog marketed the world's first commercial synthesizer, a modular system for studio work, and introduced many features that later became standard in the synthesizer. Other developments include the Minimoog, Sonic Six, Satellite, Micromoog, Polymoog, and others.

Moog filter - A filter circuit designed by Robert A. Moog.

Most significant byte - *See* **MSB**.

Motherboard - A printed circuit board into which other printed circuit boards plug. *See* **System unit.**

Mother keyboard - A keyboard that generates MIDI codes to control other instruments. Also, a master keyboard or MIDI controller.

Mouse - A device for interacting with a video screen; a small box with little wheels on the underside and a trailing cable that resembles a small mouse. As it's rolled over a flat surface, the computer counts the turns of the wheels and moves the cursor on the screen to correspond with the mouse's position.

Movieola - A projection device through which a composer can listen to music tracks while watching the picture through a glass window.

MPU401 compatible - Refers to programs capable of running with the Roland MPU401 Midi interface.

MPU401 interface - The standard MIDI interface for the IBM PC.

mS - Millisecond. A millisecond is one thousandth of a second, 1,000mS = 1 second.

MSB - Most Significant Byte - A single data byte used to represent the entire numeric range of some parameter.

MS-DOS - Microsoft Disk Operating System. A disk operating system created by the Microsoft Corporation.

MSX Standard - Licensed through Microsoft, a standard operating system for consumer computers.

MTC - MIDI Time Code. A way of synchronizing events between video devices (SMPTE) and MIDI.

MTV - Music Television. A promotional vehicle for the sale of records, formed in 1981.

Multi-mode filter - A filter that has more than one mode of operation, e.g., both lowpass and highpass, or lowpass, bandpass, band-reject, and highpass, etc.

Multiple - Found only on modular systems, a passive circuit which enables a signal or control voltage to be split and sent off to two or more other modules.

Multiple track recording - The process of recording various music elements on different tracks with the maximum amount of seperation.

Mulitiple track tape recorder - A tape recorder capable of recording or playing back three or more channels of information simultaneously.

Multiple trigger - A type of keyboard logic in which a new trigger signal is sent to the envelope generators every time a new key is depressed, whether or not a legato touch is used. Polyphonic synthesizers always operate in multiple trigger mode except when in unison mode.

Multiple-trigger keyboard response - *See* **Single/multiple trigger keyboard response.**

Multiplex - Capable of quick switching between signals.

Multiplexer - A device that takes input from several sources and delivers them in one high-speed stream of information.

Multiplexing - Sending several signals or messages at once over a single wire or communications channel.

Multi-sampling - A system allowing for different samples to be assigned to different ranges of a sampling keyboard.

Multitasking - Similar to multi-programming, except that the computer is working on several segments of the same program at once.

Multi-timbral - Capable of generating notes using two or more patches at the same time. On more complex multi-timbral instruments, each voice can be assigned its own tone color.

Multitrack MIDI sequencer - A computer program which provides similar functions as a multitrack tape recorder.

Multitrack recorder - A tape recorder that sections magnetic tape into 4, 8, 16, 24, or 32 tracks.

Multi-user - A computer that can accommodate more than one user at a time.

Musical Instrument Digital Interface - *See* **MIDI**.

Musical notation software - A computer program that allows the user to write, edit, and print music in traditional music notation.

Music Television - *See* **MTV**.

Musique Concrete - Classic tape-composition techniques as defined by Pierre Schaeffer in 1948. In this genre of electronic music, the only sound sources are recordings of ambient sounds that are then restructured and altered through the physical and electronic manipulation of the material.

Nn

NAJE - Formerly, the National Association of Jazz Educators. Effective October 1, 1989, IAJE, the International Association of Jazz Educators.

NAMM - National Association of Music Merchants.

NAND gate - An electronic circuit whose output is a "0" if all of its inputs are "1." It behaves like an AND gate hooked to an inverter.

Nano - A billionth.

Nanosecond - Particle of time equal to one billionth of a second.

National Academy of Popular Music & Songwriters Hall of Fame - NAPM.

National Academy of Recording Arts and Sciences - NARAS.

National Association of Broadcast Employees and Technicians - NABET.

National Association of Broadcasters - NAB.

National Association of Jazz Educators - Formerly NAJE, now IAJE.

National Association of Music Merchants - NAMM.

National Endowment for the Arts - NEA.

National Music Publishers Association - NMPA.

Negative feedback - Occurs when part of the signal from the output of a device, e.g., filter or amplifier, is fed back to the input, but with its polarity or phase opposite to that of the input signal.

Nest(ed) - A program within a program. Nested menus are menus that offer decision choices subsequent to original menu choices, in computers.

Nested loop - In a computer program, a loop that is contained inside another loop.

Nibble - Four of the eight bits in a byte.

Ni-cad batteries - Nickel-cadmium batteries.

Noise - Any variation in an electrical signal that is not supposed to be there. Random fluctutations in sound. *See* **Glitch.**

Noise gate - An electronic device which cuts out audio signals below a threshold selected by the engineer.

Noise generator - A device used in synthesizers for producing high frequency sound effects. *See* **White noise generator.**

Noise level - The amplitude of a noise. Usually refers to the decibel level of a steady state noise.

Noise, pink - Wide band noise that maintains constant energy per octave.

Noise, quantization - The distortion that manifests itself as a result of quantizing an analog waveform into a series of discrete voltages.

Noise reduction - The use of a compressing or expanding device which reduces unwanted tape hiss. *See* **Dolby System.**

Noise reduction system - A signal processing system designed to attenuate noise components within an audio system.

Noise, white - A wideband noise that contains equal energy at each frequency.

Non-impact printer - A printer that does not need to strike the paper to produce an image, e.g., thermal printers, electrostatic printers, and ink jet printers.

Non-inverting amplifier - An amplifier whose output signal is in phase with the input signal.

Non-parallel mixing - A type of mixing, also called series mixing, in which the two signals being added together interact to produce sidebands. This differs from ring modulation in that in non-parallel mixing the original signals are still present along with the new frequency components. *See* **Parallel mixing.**

Non-periodic - Refers to vibrations or other phenomena that do not recur at regular intervals.

Non-polarized capacitor - A can capacitor that can be utilized without regard to polarity.

Non-volatile memory - Memory in which the information is retained when the instrument is unplugged. *See* **Memory, volatile memory.**

NOR gate - An electronic circuit whose output is a "0" if any of its inputs is a "1." It behaves like an OR gate hooked to an inverter.

Normalize - To turn all of the faders, pots, switches and routing buttons completely down or to center position, on an electronic device.

Notch - A dip in frequency response at a specific frequency.

Notch filter - An electronic device which can remove unwanted frequencies with only minimal disturbance to those on either side. *See* **Filter, notch.** *See* **Band-elimination filter.**

Note off - The MIDI code that instructs an instrument to stop a note currently playing which consists of the key number, the status byte, and the velocity.

Note on - The MIDI code that instructs an instrument to play a note which consists of the key number, the status byte, and the velocity.

NTSC - National Television Standards Committee.

Number crunching - Refers to long or complex calculations.

Numbering system - Any counting system, in which a series of n digits is used to express all quantities, with base, n.

Number system, binary - n = two. *See* **Digit, binary.**

Nyquist frequency - The highest frequency that may be accurately sampled. The Nyquist frequency is one-half the sampling frequency.

Nyquist limit - The frequency above which aliasing will be introduced into a digitally generated sound.

Nyquist rate - The sampling frequency that is required in order to accurately sample all frequencies within a specified bandwidth. The Nyquist rate is twice the highest frequency which must be sampled.

Nyquist theorem - In order for a signal to be accurately reproduced, it must be sampled at a frequency which is at least higher than twice the signal's frequency.

Oo

Object code - The output of an assembler program or compiler that contains a directly executable machine language version of a program.

Octal - A number system which uses only 8 digits. Following are the numbers from 0 to 16 in decimal, octal, and binary:

Decimal	Octal	Binary
1	01	000001
2	02	000010
3	03	000011
4	04	000100
5	05	000101
6	06	000110
7	07	000111
8	10	001000
9	11	001001
10	12	001010
11	13	001011
12	14	001100
13	15	001101
14	16	001110
15	17	001111
16	20	010000

Octaphonic - A sound system with eight channels of audio information.

Octave control - A control which shifts the keyboard range up or down in octaves, on synthesizers.

OEM - Original Equipment Manufacturer. Someone who buys sub-assemblies and components and assembles them into a system for resale.

Off-line - Not connected directly to the computer system.

Off-load - To store a program on a magnetic storage device such as cassette or disk.

Offset - A user-defined fixed time interval by which a slave transport may be programmed to track the master transport. Also, a number which the computer adds to a base address to get a new effective address.

Ohm - The unit of resistance to current flow.

Ohm on mode - On MIDIs, a mode in which a receiver will respond to MIDI data on any of the 16 channels.

Omni mode - In MIDI, one of the four basic operating modes. In omni mode an instrument responds to note information received over any of MIDI's sixteen channels.

One shot - An event that has to be re-triggered every time it is required to occur.

On-line - Available, meaning that a piece of information, a program or a computer peripheral is ready to be used.

Op amp - Operational Amplifier. A wide bandwidth, high-gain amplification device.

Open - Establishing a flow of information between a file and a program so that the program can read and/or write data in the file.

Open-circuit - A broadcasting system in which any receiver within range of the broadcast station can pick up transmitted signals.

Open circuit phone jack - A jack with hot and ground connections and no switching features.

Open system - A computer that easily accomodates peripherals.

Operating system - A program which helps to overcome the problems involved in running a computer. Also called executive, monitor, or supervisor. *See* **Disk Operating System (DOS).** Also, the set of software instructions that tells a device how to respond to commands from the user.

Operational amplifier - *See* **op amp.**

Operator - A symbol which indicates an operation to be performed, such as +, -, *, etc. In Yamaha's DX series synthesizers, a term used to refer to a set of software operations that are equivalent in effect to a combination of an oscillator, a VCA, and an envelope generator.

Optical scanner - A device that reads material printed in special magnetic ink and relays the data to a computer.

Optical storage - Memory in which data is read as patterns of light.

Opto-isolator - An electronic component which combines a photoconductive device with an LED or other illuminating source.

OR - Opposite of NOR, a logic operation in which two bits or electrical pulses are combined, producing one resulting bit:

$$0 \text{ OR } 0 = 0$$
$$0 \text{ OR } 1 = 1$$
$$1 \text{ OR } 0 = 1$$
$$1 \text{ OR } 1 = 1$$

OR gate - An electronic circuit whose ouput is a "1" if any of its inputs is "1."

OS - Operating System.

OS-9 Level 2 - A multi-tasking, multi-user system for use with the Radio Shack Color Computer 3.

Oscillator (OSC) - An electronic device for generating an audio waveform. *See* **Electronic music, Square wave, Triangular wave, Sine wave, Sawtooth wave, Pulse wave, Voltage controlled oscillator.** In synthesis, the software or hardware that actually produces sound.

Oscillator drift - The tendency of an oscillator to vary slightly in frequency over long periods of time.

Oscillator sync - *See* **Sync.**

Outboard equipment (toys) - Effects devices and signal processors which are not part of a mixing console's features, e.g., flangers, harmonizers, and chorus pedals.

Output - Information produced or manipulated by a program. Also, a signal sent out by a recorder, mixer or signal processor and the point from which an audio signal leaves a recorder, mixer or signal processor.

Overall pressure sensitivity - An average pressure control signal for all keys of a keyboard being held down.

Overdrive - Distortion of an audio waveform, created by overloading an amplifier.

Overdubbing - Adding new sound to previously recorded material on a spare track, or tracks, of multitrack tape. Also, Sel-Sync.

Overflow mode - A mode of operation in which a MIDI keyboard directs all notes played simultaneously up to some maximum, to one sound-generating module and sends any notes in excess of the maximum out over MIDI.

Overlay - A system of software design which allows long programs to be written and stored on a disk ready to be called when required. In film music, a segment of music that is recorded over the original music track in order to create a special effect.

Overload - The distortion that occurs when an applied signal exceeds the level at which the system will produce its maximum output level.

Overtone - A frequency that is higher than the fundamental frequency in a sound or an audio signal.

Pp

Package - In computers, a software product designed to appeal to a wide range of data-processing customers. Also, another term for CHIP.

Page - One of a group of control-panel configurations in a digitally controlled synthesizer or computer program.

Painting notes - Drawing notes in a sequencer's graphic editor by use of a trackball, mouse, etc.

PAL - Phase Alternating Line. Acknowledged to be superior to the NTSC standard, the television and video standard for resolution, number of lines, etc., used in Europe.

Pan-pot (panoramic potentiometer) - The control knob on a recording console used for placing tracks within the stereo panorama.

Paragraphic equalizer - A graphic equalizer in which the frequency of each band is variable.

Parallel - Refers to something that transmits or processes several bits at a time, as opposed to serial operation, in which bits are handled one by one. Also, the wiring configuration in which the input leads of all devices meet at a common electrical point.

Parallel interface - An interface that can transmit many bits simultaneously over different channels or wires.

Parallel mixing - A type of mixing in which two signals are combined in such a way as not to produce any new frequency components.

Parallel port - Used by the computer to transmit information to an external device, e.g., a printer. The information is sent eight bits, or one byte, at a time. *See* **Serial.**

Parameter - A variable; a measurement. Also, data passed to a procedure or subroutine by the main program, or data produced by the procedure which it passes to the main program. Any part of a sound that can be varied to change the character of the sound, e.g., attack time, cut-off frequency, modulation index, etc.

Parameter-controlled synthesizer - A synthesizer in which the parameters are assigned identification numbers that are accessed with a number-specifying device such as a keypad.

Parametric equalizer - An equalizer which differs from a graphic equalizer in that the frequency bands selected can be continuously varied. *See* **Equalizer, parametric.**

Parity - In order to avoid PARITY ERROR, a parity bit is chosen so that the total number of 1's in a word is either even or odd. The equipment receiving the information checks the number of bits in each word to determine if an error has been made.

PASCAL - A computer language designed to teach programming in an orderly and structured manner introduced by the French mathemetician and philosopher Blaise Pascal.

Passive circuitry - A non-powered circuit.

Passive device - A network or circuit containing only passive components, such as capacitors, inductors, and resistors.

Passive radiator - *See* **Radiator, passive.**

Passport-compatible - Programs which can run with the MIDI interface for the Commodore-64.

Patch - A group of instructions that have been shoe-horned into a program to correct an error or deficiency. Also, to connect together, as the inputs and outputs of various modules, generally with patch cords. The set of parameters for a sound stored in a synthesizer's memory.

Patch bay - *See* **Jack bay.**

Patch cord - A short length of cable, with a coaxial plug on each end, used for signal routing in a jack bay.

Pattern - Also referred to as segment, a short phrase containing a rhythmic pattern with drum machines.

PC - Personal Computer.

PC board - Printed circuit board.

PC DOS - Personal Computer Disk Operating System. Distributed by IBM, a proprietary operating system for its Personal Computer line.

PCM - Pulse Code Modulation. A method for storing samples on a chip.

PCM adapter - Pulse Code Modulation adapter.

PD - Program Director.

PD synthesis - *See* **Phase distortion synthesis.**

Peak level - The highest level of the transient in any signal(s).

Peak music power - The sum amount of power that can be sent by an amplifier into a speaker at one time.

Peak-to-peak - *See* **pk-pk.**

Perf board - Perforated board. A pre-punched board to accommodate electronic components.

Performance controls - The group of controls situated close to the keyboard that are used to modify the character of the note, through a pitchbender, master volume, portamento, modulation control, etc., while it is sounding.

Period - A complete repetition of a cyclic signal.

Periodic - A regular repeating waveform thus exhibiting pitch.

Peripheral - A computer peripheral is a unit that is separate to the main computer-a printer, a disk drive, a music keyboard.

Peripheral device - Any input or output device that is attached to the system unit, e.g., a disk drive, a music keyboard, a printer, etc.

Phase - The instantaneous relationship between two measured signals when both are derived from a single, pure sine wave input.

Phase distortion - A method for generating different waveforms by distorting the synchronization of a sine wave.

Phase distortion synthesis - A form of synthesis that utilizes mathematically distorted sine waves as the basic sound source.

Phase-locking - A form of oscillator sync in which a special circuit measures the difference in frequency between the master and slave oscillators and changes the frequency of the slave so they match.

Phaser - A signal processor which produces a phasing effect.

Phase shift - The angular displacement, measured in degrees, between two sine waves of the same frequency.

Phasing - An audio effect created by simultaneously playing an identical passage on two tape recorders while slightly speeding one machine up to go out of synchronization with the other. At the point where synchronization is lost, an unusual "whooshing" sound is produced. Also called flanging.

Phone jack/plug - A 1/4-inch diameter connector used in professional studios.

Photo - Responsive to light.

Piano, electronic - A keyboard instrument whose tones are produced by reeds, strings, or other means, and amplified.

Pickup - A device that converts mechanical motion into electrical energy.

Pico - One millionth of a millionth. A trillionth.

Pink noise - A random noise signal (static) in which all frequencies above 1,000 Hz have been filtered out. Pink noise can be filtered and modulated for electronic-music purposes. *See* **Noise, Pink**. *See* **White noise, Blue noise.**

Pitch - The relative highness or lowness of a tone determined by the number of vibrations per second. Also, in film, the distance between two sprocket holes (perforations) on a strip of film.

Pitchbend - A device which enables a player to bend the pitch of a note on a synthesizer, usually with a pitch wheel, strip or lever. MIDI has a special code for sending pitch bend messages. *See* **Bend.**

Pitch-to-MIDI converter - A device that determines the frequency of an audio waveform and puts out the corresponding MIDI note data and pitch-bend data.

Pitch-to-voltage converter - A device that determines the frequency of an audio waveform and creates a control voltage that will cause the oscillator to put out its own signal at the same frequency.

Pitch transposer - *See* **Harmonizer.**

PIXEL - PIXure ELement. The smallest dot a display device can display. *See* **Resolution.**

Pk-pk - Peak to peak.

Plug - The male part of a connector pair.

Point - To adjust a computer's cursor by use of the keyboard, joystick, or mouse.

Pole - Part of a filter circuit. The more poles a low-pass filter has, the more abrupt the cutoff slope will be.

Poly - A MIDI mode that allows a synthesizer to respond to incoming MIDI messages polyphonically.

Poly-mod - Abbreviation of polyphonic modulation. Refers to a type of patch in which one audio oscillator is modulated by another, or by an envelope generator. Same as cross-mod.

Poly mode - In MIDI, one of the four basic operating modes. In poly, an instrument responds to information arriving on whatever specific numbered channel it is assigned to.

Polyphonic - Capable of producing more than one independently moving pitch line simultaneously.

Polyphonic pressure sensitivity - A keyboard function that gives aftertouch (individual pressure) data for each note played.

Polyphonic sequencer - A digital sequencer capable of storing and playing back several independent music lines simultaneously.

Polyphonic synthesizer - A synthesizer that can play more than one note at a time.

Polyphony - In electronic music, a polyphonic instrument is one that can play more than one note on the keyboard simultaneously, as opposed to monophonic systems which are limited to a single note at a time.

Polyrhythm - The use of several different rhythms simultaneously.

Polytonic - Has the capability of playing several notes at the same time.

Port - A socket, usually built into the computer, which allows information to pass in and out. MIDI uses a five-pin DIN plug.

Portamento - *See* **Glide.**

Positive feedback - Occurs when the signal that is fed back to the device from the output has the same polarity or phase as the input.

Post-score - To arrange, compose, or produce a jingle or music score after a videotape or film has been shot.

Pot - Abbreviation for potentiometer.

Potentiometer - Continuously variable level control for varying the signal in an electronic circuit; can be rotary or linear (fader). *See* **Panpot, Attenuator.**

Power amplifier -An amplifier which produces sufficient power to operate a loudspeaker.

Power consumption - The amount of wattage required by a piece of equipment.

Power supply - A circuit supplying DC power to an amplifier or other electronic system. The electronic circuits of a computer are unable to use AC voltage directly so the power supply converts it to low-voltage DC.

Power supply rejection ratio - Measured in dB, the ability of an electronic circuit to reject hums and other noises carried on the power supply line.

Ppq - Pulses per quarter note. Timing clock signals are usually sent out at a rate of 24, 48, or 96 PPQ. *See* **Resolution.**

Ppqn - *See* **Pulses per quarter note.**

Preamp - Preamplifier.

Preamplifier - An amplifier used to boost signals before they reach a main amplifier so that low level signals can be brought up to a volume that can be handled by the main amplifier.

Pre-emphasis - Record equalization.

Pre-patched - *See* **Hard-wired.**

Presets - In an electronic music instrument, predetermined sounds that can be selected through simple control-panel switches rather than through the manual use of patch cords. A simplified approach to selecting desired voices for an instrument, especially helpful with live-performance instruments.

Pressure - *See* **Aftertouch.**

Pressure sensitive - A device that provides data corresponding to the amount of pressure applied to its keys.

Pressure sensitivity - A device which enables a synthesizer to register the amount of pressure being depressed by a player on each key. *See* **Aftertouch.**

Print - Recording slang for recording a tape.

Print buffer - *See* **Print spooler.**

Printed circuit - A thin layer of copper, bonded to an insulating board made of phenolic or fiberglass, is immersed in a chemical etching bath. After the copper is dissolved away, areas which have been coated with a material that resists the action of the etchant remain and form the wiring of the circuit.

Printer - A hardware component capable of converting data from a computer into printed form.

Print-out - Printed data produced by a computer.

Print spooler - Also called print buffer, a computer memory that retains data to be printed so that other tasks can be accomplished while printing is taking place.

Print-through - The transfer of a signal from one layer of magnetic tape to an adjacent layer.

Priority - *See* **Assignment priority.**

Processor - The hardware component of the computer that actually performs the computations by directly executing instructions stored in the computer's main memory.

Producer - The person who is responsible for organizing, hiring and firing, and all creative decisions in music productions, video or film, radio or television.

Production - The recording of music and/or video taping or filming.

Production studio - A fully-equipped audio recording studio which prepares master tapes for sales and presentations of music which has previously been recorded at another location.

Program - A series of coded instructions that tell the computer what to do. In synthesizers, to create a new sound through front-panel settings, or through an input to a signal processor that causes the processor to act on another input in a way specified by the program. To edit a patch or to enter data.

Program chain - A pre-selected series of patch programs that can be called up one after another, usually with a foot switch. *See* **Chain.**

Program change - The MIDI code that instructs an instrument to select one of its patch memories so it can be played.

Programmable - A synthesizer that contains a computer memory which allows the user to store a number of aspects of a patch and recall them simultaneously to active status by touching a separate memory control section.

Programmed music - The generation of music by means of automatic high-speed digital computers.

Programmer - A person who writes directions for the sequential behavior of an electronic system, e.g., a computer.

Programming language - A system of symbols used to give instructions to a computer. Synonymous with high-level language.

PROM - Programmable Read Only Memory.

Prompt - An onscreen indicator that indicates MS-DOS is waiting for instructions. The MS-DOS prompt consists of the default drive letter (usually A,B, or C) and >. An example of an MS-DOS prompt is A>.

Psychoacoustics - The study of the brain's perception of, and reaction to, all aspects of sound.

Psychophysics - The study of the relationship between physical stimuli and the brain's interpretation of them.

Pull-down menu - In computers, usually overlaying the present contents of the screen without disrupting them; a set of choices for actions that appears near the top of a display screen.

Pull-down resistor - A resistor that connects from a signal line to ground.

Pull-up resistor - A resistor that connects from a signal line to a positive voltage reference.

Pulse - A sudden and abrupt jump in an electrical quantity from its usual level to a lower or higher value, followed by an abrupt return.

Pulses per quarter note - The number of clock sync pulses generated during a quarter note by a drum machine, sequencer, etc.

Pulse wave - A waveform produced by sudden voltage changes from negative to positive to negative. Also, a waveshape generated by an oscillator consisting of an alternating high and low steady state voltage.

Pulse width - *See* **Duty cycle.**

Pulse-width modulation - A voltage-controlled change in the width of a pulse wave.

Punch in - The system in recording whereby a fresh part is added to existing material on tape by switching from play to record while the tape is moving.

Punch out - Leave the recording process after a punch in.

Pure tone - A single frequency sine wave, with no harmonics present.

PWM - Pulse Width Modulation. Varying the width of a pulse wave over time which changes its timbre.

PZM - Pressure Zone Microphone - A Crown microphone which is insensitive to receiving multiple out-of-phase signals from an acoustic sound source.

Qq

Q - In a bandpass equalizer, the ratio of center frequency to bandwidth. *See* **Resonance.**

Quad - *See* **Quadrasonic sound reproduction.**

Quadrophonic - *See* **Quadrasonic sound reproduction.**

Quadrophonic sound - Four-way sound that reaches the listener from every side with instruments positioned all around the panorama. *See* **Panning.**

Quadrophonic sound reproduction - A system of sound reproduction involving four speakers, each operating from its own channel.

Quantization - The noise which occurs in digital sound reproduction when numerical expressions of sound are rounded off to their nearest numerical equivalent. Quantization of an audio signal is called digitization or digital-to-analog conversion. *See* **Quantized, Auto-correct, Digital-to-analog converter,** etc.

Quantization noise - *See* **Noise, quantization.**

Quantize - Used by most drum machines and sequencers, the rounding off of rhythmic values to a particular value, e.g., eighth or sixteenth notes, used to correct rhythmic errors. *See* **Auto-correct.**

Quantized - Set up to produce an output in discrete steps. In most digital and analog-digital hybrid instruments, all front panel-knobs and sliders are quantized.

Quantizer - A module that accepts an incoming voltage and matches this as closely as possible at its output while confining the output to one of a series of equally spaced discrete steps.

Quasi-parametric - A filter section resembling a parametric equalizer but has no bandwidth control.

Quick disk - A form of fast memory storage like a floppy disk, but read sequentially rather than in a random access manner.

QWERTY keyboard - The standard typewriter-computer keyboard.

Rr

Radiator, passive - An unpowered loud speaker cone, placed in the port of a vented enclosure system. Also called a slave cone or a drone cone.

RAM - *See* **Random access memory.**

RAM cache - *See* **Cache.**

RAM cartridge - A device which plugs into a computer port or synthesizer and contains RAM.

Ramp wave - *See* **Sawtooth wave.**

RAM resident - *See* **Memory-resident.**

Random access - A computer system in which the time necessary to store and retrieve information is independent of the storage location. Same as direct access.

Random access memory (RAM) - Memory available for the temporary storage of programs and date. Any information in RAM is destroyed when you turn off the system unit's power.

Random generator - An electronic device that produces all frequencies in the sound spectrum simultaneously with a random frequency and amplitude pattern.

Rate level EG - An envelope generator in which the envelope shape is defined in terms of an ordered set of pairs of numbers. Casio CZ-101 and Yamaha DX7 use rate-level envelope generators.

Rate scaling - *See* **Envelope tracking.**

RCA phone jack/plug - *See* **Phono jack/plug.**

R-DAT - Recording Digital Audio Tape. A digital audio tape recorder that uses rotating head technology.

Read - When a disk drive retrieves data from a disk, the computer is said to be "reading" information. Also, playback (read head = playback head).

Read only memory (ROM) - Memory that permanently stores information that was built into the computer during its manufacture. You can access this section of memory and read its contents, but you cannot alter it. The information is not destroyed when the power is turned off.

Readout - An electronic component that displays information.

Read/write - A storage device into which new data may be written or from which data may be read.

Real-time - Live; happening now. A live performance. When a computer plays a program it is playing non-real-time music.

Real-time messages - *See* **System real-time.**

Real-time mode - The opposite of single-step mode, a situation in which events are entered in computer memory at a speed proportional to the speed at which they will be played back.

Real-time recording - The uninterrupted recording of continuous action and sound, usually as relates to videotape recording.

Regeneration - *See* **Resonance.**

Regulator - *See* **Voltage regulator.**

Release - The last in the four parameters of an envelope generator, or ADSR.

Release velocity - The speed with which a key is raised after being depressed.

Remanence - The magnetization left on a tape when a magnetic force is removed. Remanence is measured in lines of flux per quarter inch of tape width.

Remote keyboard - A keyboard module that is not built into the same housing as the tone-generating circuitry it controls.

Removable media - Data storage media that can be removed from the drive that reads/writes it, e.g., floppy disks and magnetic tape.

Requester box - The dialog box on the Amiga computer.

Reset - *See* **System reset.**

Reset-switch - A switch found on microcomputers which wipes out all RAM and resets the computer to an empty mode.

Resistance - The opposition of a circuit to a flow of direct current. Resistance is measured in ohms.

Resistor - An electronic component that opposes current flow.

Resolution - The fineness of detail visible in a display or printout. Also, the fineness of the divisions into which analog input is digitized or into which real-time input is quantized for memory storage. In MIDI, the number of increments into which a drum machine or sequencer divides a beat.

Resonance - The condition of a system when the applied frequency is equal to the natural frequency of vibration of the system. Filter resonance, also known as emphasis, feedback, regeneration, and Q, is a mode of operation in which a narrow band of frequencies becomes relatively more prominent.

Resynthesis - The process of electronically approximating the sound of an acoustic instrument by analyzing its frequency and amplitude components and then using the information to control the operation of a synthesizer voice.

Retrofit - Adding new capabilities or functions to equipment.

Reverb - *See* **Reverberation.**

Reverberation - An electronic effect used to add depth and resonance to a sound, typically generated by running an audio signal through a spring device that adds a slight delay to the sound of the original signal. Also, the sound characteristics of a room.

Reverse video - Reversing the color of objects on a field, e.g., white on black, etc.

RFI - Radio Frequency Interference.

RF modulator - A circuit which converts video signals from a computer to high frequencies for interfacing with a TV.

RGB - Red, Green, Blue. The three primary colors in color picture tubes.

RGB output - The connector that emits discrete signals to control the RGB in a color monitor.

Ribbon - A controller most often used for pitchbending.

Ribbon controller - A linear controller through which pitch can be continuously varied by sliding a finger along a band of metal or pressure-sensitive strip.

Ringing - A carry-over effect sometimes generated by electrical components as they continue to respond to signals that have ended. *See* **Resonance.**

Ring modulator - Used as sound modifiers in electronic music composition, ring modulators are electronic devices which accept two channels of input and feeds the sum and output of the different frequencies to a single frequency.

RISC - Reduced Instruction Set Computer. A computer designed to execute instructions quickly.

Rise time - The time between the beginning of a sound and the point at which it reaches maximum amplitude.

Roll off - To reduce high frequencies. Also, the rate at which a signal is attenuated by a filter.

Rolloff slope - The acuity of the cutoff frequency. When the rolloff slope is shallow (6dB per octave) the frequency components beyond the cutoff frequency can still be heard, but at a volume reduced in proportion to how far past the cutoff frequency they are. When the rolloff slope is steep (24dB per octave) frequency components close to the cutoff frequency are so reduced in volume as to fall below the threshold of audibility.

ROM - *See* **Read only memory.**

ROM cartridge - A plug-in device that contains ROM.

Rotating head - Magnetic heads in which the playback and record rotate on an axis.

Round-off error - The mistake which may occur when the computer produces more digits in a result than can be used.

Routing - *See* **Assigning.**

RS-232 - The most widely used standard for serial data transmission.

RS-422 - A serial computer interface which is faster than the RS-232.

Run - To execute a program.

Running status- In many MIDI devices, a technique used to reduce the number of bytes needed to send MIDI messages.

Ss

Sample - A digitally recorded and stored representation of a sound.

Sample-and-hold - A device that samples an incoming voltage to determine its level, and puts out a signal at that level until the next time it is told to take a sample, regardless of what the incoming voltage has been doing in the meantime.

Sample dump standard - A system exclusive format for MIDI samplers to exchange their memory with other samplers or with computers through MIDI.

Sample length - In seconds or milliseconds, the length of a sample.

Sampler - A digital device capable of sampling. *See* **Sample**. Also, a keyboard or rack-mount module that records and plays back digital representations of acoustic sounds.

Sample rate - *See* **Sampling rate.**

Sampling - The process of examining an analog signal at regular intervals, which are defined by the sampling rate. Also, a form of synthesis based on an existing sound. A sound is digitally encoded in the memory of the instrument and this data is manipulated so as to provide the sound at different pitches across the span of the keyboard or controller.

Sampling frequency - The frequency at which the analog signal is sampled, usually expressed in hertz. *See* **Sampling rate.**

Sampling rate - In music applications, the rate at which a computer measures sound. For professional fidelity, the sampling rates chosen by the recording industry are between 40,000 and 50,000 times per second.

Save - To save a program or file from main memory to a peripheral device such as a disk drive.

Sawtooth wave - A waveform containing the fundamental frequency and all of its overtones with the amplitude of each overtone inversely proportional to its position in the harmonic series.

Scale mode - A control mode that allows the user to alter the pitches of individual keys on the keyboard in relation to one another.

Scaling - The distance between colors and sounds that can be measured by a computer analysis of data.

Scaling curve - A user-defined non-linear relationship between input and output.

Schmitt trigger - A device that puts out a pulse whenever the input voltage it is sensing rises above a certain threshold.

Screen dump - A printout of data displayed on a computer screen at the time of initiating the screen dump command.

Screen message - Text that appears on the monitor screen to instruct you to type an entry or press a key.

SCSI - Small Computer System Interface. Hardware/software protocol for transmitting data between computers or peripherals and computers.

S-DAT - A digital tape recorder which uses stationary head technology.

Second touch - Same as aftertouch in that it comprises an additional control signal that is applied from the keyboard to a sound while a key is still being held down by exerting extra pressure.

Sector - The surface of a magnetic disk is divided up into a series of wedge-shaped segments called sectors.

Segment - *See* **Pattern.**

Self-oscillation - *See* **Resonance.**

Semiconductor - The heart of the computer. A material with an electrical conductivity somewhere between a good conductor (metal) and a poor conductor (insulating material).

Sequence - A set of voltages or keystroke commands and other data stored in a sequencer. Also, a section or unit of music.

Sequencer - A device for generating a repeatable series of control voltages for the triggering of tonal or percussive sounds in a synthesizer. Sequencers may be analog or digital in design. In MIDI, a device that records MIDI events. *See* **Analog sequencer, Digital sequencer, Polyphonic sequencers, etc.**

Sequencer file format - A format used for digitally storing data concerning sequences.

Sequential memory - *See* **Random access.**

Serial - Something that transmits or processes a series of bits one at a time, as opposed to parallel operation, in which several bits are handled at once.

Serial interface - An interface where data is transmitted one bit at a time over a single channel or wire. Also, a connection between two devices in which digital information is transferred one bit after another, rather than several bits at a time, e.g., MIDI.

Serial port - Used by the computer to transmit information to an external device, such as a printer or modem. The information is sent one bit at a time.

SFX - Abbreviation for special effects.

S/H - Sample-and-hold.

Shareware - Software which is shared.

Shepard function generator - A circuit that produces the illusion of a constant falling and rising group of tones.

Short circuit - When two conductors connect the sound ceases or the amp is destroyed.

SID chip - Sound Interface Device chip used in the Commodore-64 computer.

Sidebands - Frequency components outside the natural harmonic series introduced to the tone by using audio-range wave for modulation.

Signal chain - The processing stages of a signal going through a system.

Signal processing device - An audio system used to modify some characteristic of the signal passing through it.

Signal-to-noise ratio - The ratio of the signal voltage to the noise voltage, usually expressed as the decibel difference.

Silicon - One of the most important natural materials applied in technology. A perfect semiconductor and the material from which most microprocessors are constructed.

Sine wave - The waveform of a single frequency. Also, a signal put out by an oscillator in which the voltage rises and falls smoothly and symmetrically, following the formula of the sine function in trigonometry.

Single-ended noise reduction - A noise reduction system which processes an incoming signal allowing for the processed output to occur simultaneously with the input.

Single in-line package - *See* **SIP.**

Single/multiple trigger keyboard response- In single trigger response, a new envelope is triggered only if no other keys are held; in multiple triggering, every time a new key is played, an envelope is generated.

Single-sided - A disk which can only be written to or read from one side.

Single step mode - A method of loading events into memory one event at a time, which usually entails separately entering information about the time of the events. *See* **Real-time mode.**

Single trigger - A type of keyboard logic sometimes found on monophonic synthesizers and on polyphonic synthesizers in unison mode, in which a new trigger signal is sent to the envelope generators only after an interval of time in which no key was depressed.

SIP - Single In-line Package. A packaging, where all pins are arranged in a single row, for IC's and other components.

Sixteen(16)-bit - The bit size in computer measurement refers to the number of bits that can move through a computer at once. Microprocessors are designed as 8-bit or 16-bit units. At this time, although 32-bit systems are being developed, most music computers are using 8-bit technology.

Slave - Any device whose operation is linked to and governed by some other device called a master, e.g., master oscillator, master keyboard, etc. A MIDI device that is controlled by another MIDI device.

Slave device - A device that is under the control of a master device, in MIDI.

Slide pot - A pot (potentiometer) which has a knob moving linearly to make changes rather than one which turns.

Slope - The fourth segment of Korg's six-stage envelope generators, which determine the speed at which the envelope will fall or rise from the break point to the sustain level.

Slots - Mounted on a motherboard, connectors for receiving computer peripherals.

Smart MIDI interface - A MIDI interface that includes internal software and a microprocessor.

SMPTE - Society of Motion Picture and Television Engineers. SMPTE is used to describe the timing standard adopted to synchronize tape decks, video playback devices, and other equipment used in video or movie production.

SMPTE code - Defined by the Society of Motion Picture & Television Engineers, a standard protocol used for synchronizing various devices, e.g., motion picture projectors, tape recorders, and videotape players.

SMPTE time code - *See* **Time code, SMPTE.**

Soft - A music instrument which is computer-based and peforms according to software instructions.

Software - Programs that run on computer hardware. Software consists of coded instructions for the computer to follow; a sample of a sound on a disk, music on a tape or record, the codes inside the chips in instruments, etc.

Software gap - The gap between the capabilities of hardware and the programmers.

Solid-state - Electrical circuit built without electro-mechanical parts, e.g., tubes (valves). Transistor circuitry.

Song - A list of drum machine or sequencer patterns that the machine will play back in the desired order.

Song position pointer (SPP) - A type of MIDI data that tells a device how many sixteenth-notes into a song to begin its playback.

Song select - A MIDI code used to instruct drum machines or sequencers which song in their memory to play.

Source - A noise source, oscillator, or external input that serves as the point of origin of the audio signal path.

Source code - The input text file for an assembler, compiler, or inter-preter.

Spectrum analyzer - Test equipment that shows the amount of energy present in frequency bands across the electromagnetic spectrum.

Speech-analyzer - A system that can recognize spoken words and transform them to computer commands.

Spike - A brief high-voltage transient that occurs on an AC power line.

Split - Multiplying a signal into two or more outputs.

Split keyboard - A single keyboard which is divided electronically to emulate two separate manuals, with the output of each half being routed into a separate signal path.

Split point - The point at which a split keyboard is split.

Square wave - A waveform comprised of a fundamental sinewave frequency and its odd-numbered harmonics. Also, a pulse wave with a 50% duty cycle.

SRAM - *See* **Static RAM.**

SSDD - Single-Sided, Double-Density. A former disk format that recorded data on one side at double density.

SSSD - Single-Sided, Single-Density. A disk format that records data on one side at single density.

Standard pitch - A1 = 440 vibrations per second was unanimously adopted as the standard pitch in May,1939 at the International Conference on Pitch held in London.

Standby power supply - A supply that activates when a power failure has occurred. This supply is similar to a UPS but power is normally supplied by the incoming AC signal.

Star network - A way of interconnecting equipment with all signals coming from a central point to the other system elements.

Start - The MIDI code which tells a drum machine or sequencer to play a song from the beginning.

State-variable filter - A filter whose response characteristics can be varied, e.g., from lowpass to bandpass to highpass, etc.

Static filter - A filter whose characteristics remain fixed once set by the front panel controls.

Static RAM - RAM that requires no renewing to retain data.

Status bytes - Usually followed by one or more data bytes, a code that defines the kind of information being sent in a MIDI message.

Step input - *See* **Single-step mode.**

Step programming - Programming and editing on a synthesizer one function at a time, using common entry keys or programming a drum machine or sequencer one measure at a time, as opposed to playing into it live.

Step time - The division of note lengths into equal units of time.

Stereo - *See* **Stereophonic sound.**

Stereophonic - An audio system which reproduces spatial information, giving the listener the illusion of width and depth.

Stereophonic sound - Sound reproduction using two or more channels which recreate the effect of the original performance, spatially and in terms of highs and lows.

Stick - *See* **Chapman stick.**

Stop - The MIDI code which tells a drum machine or sequencer to stop playing.

Storage - An electronic device that accepts data and stores it until the data is needed and retrieved. *See* **Buffer, Computer, Disk storage, Memory.**

Store - *See* **Save.**

S-trigger gate - As opposed to a logic level signal, a gate signal resulting from a switch closure.

String - A string of numbers or letters grouped together; usually in a computer program.

Stripe - To record SMPTE time code on tape.

Stripe a tape - To record SMPTE time code from the beginning to the end of the tape.

Stripe card reader - A device that decodes information contained in a strip of magnetic tape usually embedded in a plastic card.

Sub-audio - The lower threshold of human hearing or below about 20 Hz.

Subcode - A subset of a CD's data frame that contains 8 bits: P, Q, R, S, T, U, V, and W.

Sub-octave generator - A circuit that puts out a signal whose frequency is equal to the frequency of the input signal divided by some integer, usually two.

Sub-oscillator - In some synthesizers, an additional tone generator located one, two, or more octaves below the main oscillator.

Subroutine - A secondary part of a computer program which is called up during program operation to carry out a specific task.

Subtractive synthesis - The modification of electronic sounds through the rejection or filtering of given overtones or frequency ranges.

SuperBeta - A Beta video recording technology with an improved audio and about a 20% improvement in picture quality over the standard Beta.

Support circuitry - Extra parts in a major integrated circuit to make it complete.

Surge - A sudden increase in power line voltage.

Surge suppressor - An instrument that absorbs voltage surges.

Sustain - A level control and the third of the four segments controlled by an ADSR envelope generator. The sustain portion of the envelope begins when the attack and decay portions have run their course and continues until the key is released. In MIDI, a controller that causes notes to hold after NOTE OFF commands have been received.

Sustain pedal - The electronic equivalent of a piano's damper pedal.

Sustain switch - A switch on synthesizers that simulates holding down the pedal on an acoustic piano.

S-VHS - An improved videotape format.

Switch controller - *See* **Continuous controllers.**

Switching power supply - A heavy duty power supply characterized by little heat dissipation and efficient operation.

Switch trigger - A type of trigger signal that consists of a sudden, brief drop in voltage. *See* **Voltage trigger**.

Sync - Synchronize or synchronization. Two devices, such as arpeggiators, drum machines, or sequencers are synced when the clock output of one is patched to the external clock input of the other, so that the timing of the notes they play will be coordinated.

Sync block - In films, a device used to keep film and sprocketed wound tracks in sync, in editing.

Synchronization - *See* **Sync.**

Synchronizer - *See* **Sync block.**

Synchro-sonic - A recording technique in which non-percussive instruments are made to sound drum-like.

Synclavier - A polyphonic digital synthesizer, manufactured by the New England Digital Corporation of White River Junction, Vermont and developed by Sydney Alonso, Cameron Jones, and Jon Appleton in 1972. Based on the computer-controlled Dartmouth Digital Synthesizer, it allows detailed control of waveshape generation by direct video-monitor interface and other systems. A "tapeless" recording studio, it can record complete multi-track masters on hard disk.

Sync track - A timing reference signal recorded on tape which is intended to be patched directly to devices, e.g., drum machines and sequencers, that will accept the appropriate clock input.

Synergistic - Greater than the sum of its parts.

Synth - Synthesizer.

Synthesizer - A self-contained instrument designed for the generation, modification, amplification, mixing, and presentation of electronic sounds.

Sysex - System Exclusive Messages.

System common messages - MIDI messages used to enhance the functions of other commands, e.g., song position pointer, song select, tune request, etc.

System-exclusive - MIDI data whose format is specified by an individual manufacturer. Such data is used for transmitting sound parameter changes, patch memory contents, and sound samples from one digital device to another.

System exclusive messages - MIDI codes for sending data for a specific instrument.

System message - A type of message received by MIDI devices in a MIDI network without regard for the MIDI channel the devices are set to receive.

System real-time - MIDI data, including clock data, active sensing, and start, stop, and continue messages.

System real-time message - A type of system message that synchronizes performance timing among devices, in MIDI.

System reset - To clear the computer's memory and reload the operating system by pressing the reset button (on some computers) or simultaneously pressing CTRL, ALT, and DEL. Sometimes called a warm boot. Also, the MIDI command that returns instruments to the condition they were in when first turned on.

Systems software - All the programs that tie together and coordinate the devices that make up the computer system, e.g., compilers, input/ output routines, and loaders.

System unit - The main component of a computer, usually separate from the monitor and keyboard. The system unit is where the actual manipulation and storage of data take place.

Tt

Tach pulse - Tachometer pulse. On some tape recorders, a signal that correlates to transport motor movement and the amount of tape sent from one reel to another.

Tape delay - A method for recording sounds in real time and replaying them after regularly spaced intervals. This is done using a single loop of tape that is threaded through the record head of one tape machine and the playback head of another. The distance between the two heads determines the length of the delay that will occur.

Tape echo - A means of delaying the repeat of a sound by adjusting the time lapse or delay between the record and playback heads of a tape recorder. Also called a tape slap.

Tape loop - A single piece of magnetic tape, spliced end to end. Loops are used to repeat sound patterns over and over upon playback or in tape-delay configurations in real time.

Tape recorder - An electronic device which converts sound into electrical energy for storage on magnetic tape and then re-converts the electrical energy into sound. *See* **Multiple-track tape recorder, Four-track tape recorder, Two-track tape recorder, Full-track tape recorder, Quarter-track tape recorder.**

Telecommunications - Using telephone circuits, voice and/or data communications.

Teletype (TTY) - A computer terminal resembling a large typewriter which provides a printed record of information that passes between the computer and the user.

Terminal - A device used to receive and transmit information in a computer. Also, a device at the end of an electrical wire that is used as a connector into a circuit.

Text file - A collection of data representing words.

THD - Total Harmonic Distortion. The sum of all harmonic distortion components in a signal.

3 dB point - The point at which amplitude has decreased to 3 dB less than a specific reference point, with frequency response.

Throughput - The total volume of work performed by a computer in a given period of time.

Thru box - In MIDI, an accessory that turns a single MIDI In into several MIDI Out signals which have the same data as the MIDI In.

Timbre - The quality or nature of a sound, sometimes known as tone color in music. It distinguishes one voice or patch from another.

Time code, SMPTE - The time-code standard, as adopted by the SMPTE, in which each recorded tape segment is assigned a unique 80-bit digital word code, defining the hour, minute, second and frame number at which that segment of tape was recorded.

Time-correct - *See* **Auto-correct.**

Time slot - The specific time at which a radio or television program is scheduled to begin and end.

Timing clock - The system real time message, sent 24 times per beat, used to synchronize devices.

Tin - The thin coat of solder over a wire before soldering.

Title bar - Also called a menu bar, the configuration that comes up on the computer screen which lists the title for the menus in a program.

Tolerance rating - The tested and assigned rating for capacitors and resistors.

Tone mix - A Casio term to refer to internal two-voice layering.

TOS - Tramiel Operating System. The operating system used in Atari ST computers.

Touch pad - Also called a touch plate, a controller that senses the presence of a finger and puts out corresponding control voltages.

Touch pad/switch - A control that has no moving parts, but is activated by touch. It can be used to switch any parameter that is controlled by a mechanical switch.

Touch responsive - A control that has no moving parts, but is activated by touch. It can be used to switch any parameter that is controlled by a mechanical switch.

Touch-sensitive - Pressure with corresponding variations in a control signal output that is separate from the main output of the module or equipped with a sensing mechanism that responds to variations in velocity. Also, aftertouch, velocity sensitivity.

TPI - The number of tracks on a floppy disk per each inch of radius.

Trace - In computers, a debugging aid which gives the programmer a record of the contents of the program counter and the main registers after each instruction is executed.

Track - A division of a disk. Each disk is divided into a specified number of tracks, which are further subdivided into a certain number of sectors. A doubled-sided floppy disk has 80 or more tracks, a 10-megabyte fixed disk has over 1200, and a 20-megabyte fixed disk contains over 2400. Also, a specific and continuous area of magnetic tape or film which contains recorded information, derived from a single electronic channel. In sequencers, one of a number of independent memory banks. *See* **Tape recorder, Multiple-track recording.**

Trackball - A fist-sized ball, mounted to spin freely in any direction and used to communicate with a computer through a video display.

Tracks - A term sometimes used by companies producing soft instruments to describe a multiple sequencer. Also, the recorded paths on a magnetic recording tape. In digital recording, a single audio channel may require more than one recorded track on a digital tape recorder. *See* **Basic tracks.**

Tracking - The ability of a meter movement, or other dynamic device to precisely follow the envelope of the applied waveform. The process of completing a recording session track by track, as in a Sel-Sync session.

Track shift - Sliding a sequencer track backward or forward in time.

Transducer - A device which converts energy from one form to another.

Transient - A relatively high amplitude, suddenly decaying, peak signal level.

Transient generator - An electronic device used to duplicate the attack sounds of music instruments. *See* **Transient overtones, Envelope generator.**

Transistor - An electronic device used in a circuit to amplify, or modify in some other way the flow of current. *See* **Solid-state.**

Transistor-transistor logic - TTL.

Transparent - In computers, refers to something the equipment does that the user is not aware of.

Tremolo - A rapid variation in the amplitude of a single pitch. *See* **Amplitude modulation.**

Triangular wave - A waveform containing the fundamental frequency and odd numbered harmonics which decrease in amplitude rapidly in relation to their distance from the fundamental. Also, a signal put out by an oscillator that rises and then falls smoothly and linearly.

Trigger - To activate, to set off, to start. A trigger into an analog input causes the relevant note to sound. Also, a signal used to initiate an electronic process, e.g., the switching OFF or ON of an oscillator in synthesizer.

Truncation - If there are too many digits in a number for the computer to represent it properly, the extra digits are chopped off and eliminated. *See* **Round-off error.**

TTL - Transistor-transistor logic.

TTL-compatible - Hardware which can interface with TTL devices.

Tune request - The MIDI command that causes analog synthesizers to retune their oscillators.

Twelve-bit - Using twelve-bit digital words to process and/or store data.

Two-pole - *See* **Pole, roll off.**

Uu

U - A unit of measurement, 1.75 inches in height, for rack-mount panels.

UART - Universal Asynchronous Receiver/Transmitter. In computers, an integrated circuit in which one half converts parallel data into serial form and the other half performs the reverse operation.

UHF - Ultra High Frequency. Television broadcast frequencies, channels 14 and up, reserved by the FCC for local and community-access stations.

Ultrasonic - Above the range of human hearing (frequencies over 20,000 Hz).

Unbalanced line - A line consisting of two conductors, one of which is at ground potential. The unbalanced line is often in the form of a single conductor plus shield, with the shield serving as the second conductor.

Undefined status bytes - Bytes for which no corresponding MIDI messages exist.

Unimplemented status bytes - Part of the MIDI specification but not implemented.

Uninterruptible power supply - *See* **UPS.**

Unipolar - A power supply voltage within a single polarity range.

Unison - When two or more oscillators are running at the same frequency. Also, when all the voices on a polyphonic instrument are assigned to a single key.

Unison mode - A keyboard logic in which several or all of an instrument's voices are activated by a single key.

Unix - A mini-computer operating system developed at Bell Laboratory in which programs can be connected by "pipes" so that the output of one program becomes the input of the next.

Upload - To send data from a computer to another computer, disk drive, electronic mail service, etc.

UPS - Uninterruptible Power Supply. A device that keeps a computer running through brief power outages.

Upward compatible - When a piece of equipment can do everything the previous model could and more, it is "upward compatible".

User - The person operating the computer, usually when a program is running.

User-friendly - Applied to program design. A user-friendly program or system is one that makes operation easy for unskilled operators.

User interface - Methods, displays, and controls through which a user interacts with a computer, device, or instrument.

Utilities - Basic programs in a computer system, e.g., DOS and languages.

Utility program - Computer programs made available by the operating system to save programmers the bother of writing their own programs to do often needed tasks.

Vv

Valve - Vacuum tube.

VAR - Value-Added Reseller.

Variable - In computers, an area in memory to which you have given a name. Also, a control parameter that is continuously variable, i.e., one that is not just on or off, nor quantized.

Variac - The trade name for a specific variable transformer.

VCA - *See* **Voltage-controlled amplifier.**

VCF - *See* **Voltage-controlled filter.**

VCO - *See* **Voltage-controlled oscillator.**

VCR - Video Cassette Recorder. A device that stores video signals on magnetic tape.

VCS3 synthesizer - Manufactured by EMS, a synthesizer which includes a pin matrix. Also called the Putney.

VDP - Video Disc Player.

VDT - Video Display Terminal.

VDU - Visual Display Unit. VDU's are intended for business use and display 80 characters horizontally against the more normal 40 characters found on micro-computer screens.

Velocity - The speed with which a drum pad, key, or string is hit or released, in MIDI.

Velocity data - MIDI data conventionally used to indicate how hard a key was struck.

Velocity-sensitive keyboard - A music keyboard that senses the speed of its keys when they are pressed or released.

Velocity sensitivity - Touch sensitivity in which the keyboard measures how fast the key is descending while it is still in motion, or how hard it initially strikes the key bed.

Vernier - A pot used for fine tuning.

VES - Visual Editing System. A system that displays waveforms of audio samples stored in a sampling machine.

VHF - Very High Frequency. The band of television broadcast frequencies, channels 2 through 13, reserved by the FCC for networks and their local affiliates.

VHS - Video Home System.

VHS Hi-Fi - VHS with improved audio quality.

Vibrato - A rapid fluctuation in the pitch of a note. *See* **Frequency modulation.**

Video cassette recorder - *See* **VCR.**

Video monitor - *See* **Display.**

Vocalizer 1000 - A device with small speaker, which can also be plugged into a home stereo, boom box or guitar amplifier. When hummed into the microphone, a digitally sampled sound is converted into a saxophone, trumpet, guitar, etc.; a total of 28 different sounds. Developed by Breakaway Music Systems in 1989, it includes MIDI pots for linking to other synthesizers, sequencers and computers.

Vocoder - An electronic-music device designed for analyzing and synthesizing sounds and to modulate the sound of the human voice. It was developed by Homer Dudley in 1936 at the Bell Telephone Laboratories in Murray Hill, New Jersey. The Vocoder continuously analyzes the frequency spectrum of one incoming signal and imparts analogous spectral characteristics to another.

Voice - The output of a single audio signal path, or a response from an instrument that acts as if it were coming from such an output.

Voice assignment - *See* **Assignment priority.**

Voice messages - Messages that control an instrument's voice, in MIDI.

Voice module - The combined forces of oscillators, filters, amplifiers, envelope generators, low frequency oscillators. All the blocks that are used to make a synthesized sound can be considered a voice module.

Voiceprinting - Computerized analysis of a human voice to detect individual voice characteristics.

Voice recognition - Computers can recognize individual words, by extensive analysis of speech, and respond to them as data or commands.

Voice synthesizer - A computer output device that simulates a human voice.

Volatile memory - In computers, a memory whose information vanishes when the power is turned off.

Voltage - The difference in potential between two points in an electrical circuit.

Voltage control - In electronic music synthesizers, the use of DC voltages to activate and regulate the generation of sound. Voltage-controlled synthesizers use oscillators, amplifiers, filters, and other components that can be controlled in this way. *See* **Voltage-controlled oscillator, Voltage-controlled amplifier, Voltage-controlled filter.**

Voltage-controlled amplifier (VCA) - An amplifier component of a synthesizer that can be controlled with voltage inputs.

Voltage-controlled attenuator - A resistive network, or an amplifier whose gain is less than unity, whose attenuation is a function of an externally-supplied (DC) control voltage.

Voltage-controlled filter (VCF) - A filtering component of a synthe-sizer that can be controlled with voltage inputs.

Voltage-controlled mixer - A device for combining several input sig-nals, whose degree of amplification may be varied by means of change in control voltage.

Voltage-controlled oscillator (VCO) - An oscillator component of a synthesizer that can be controlled with voltage inputs.

Voltage follower - A buffer circuit with lower-impedance stage.

Voltage pedal - A foot-operated control voltage source.

Voltage regulator - A device that provides constant output voltage.

Voltage trigger - A trigger signal that consists of a sudden, brief increase in voltage. *See* **Switch trigger.**

Volt-per-octave - The number of volts required to shift the pitch of an oscillator one octave in voltage controlled systems.

Volume - The effect caused by the amplitude of the sound wave. The greater the displacement, the greater the volume or intensity, and vice versa. In MIDI, the code used to adjust the overall output level of an instrument.

VTR - Video Tape Recorder. *See* **VCR.**

Ww

Wah-wah pedal - A pedal which produces a "wah" effect by sweeping the tone from bass to treble and back. *See* **Wa-wa**.

Warm start - The process of restarting a computer after the power has already been turned on, usually without re-loading the program or DOS and often without losing the data and program currently in the computer.

Watt - A unit of power.

Wave - As in sound wave. The shape of the graph (wave-like) that represents the frequency of a sound.

Waveform - A graph of a signal's amplitude vs. time. The waveform of a pure tone is a sine wave. In synthesis, common waveforms are pulse, sawtooth, square, and triangle.

Waveform memory - A computer memory device, either RAM or ROM, which holds all of the information pertaining to a waveform.

Waveform modulation - A voltage-controlled change in the shape of the wave an oscillator is putting out, independent of any change in its frequency.

Waveform table - A method of arranging information about a waveform that sets it out as a table in computer memory allowing the user rapid access to any part of the information.

Wave shape - Waves produced by each type of instrument giving it its quality. *See* **Waveform.**

Wavetable - The set of numbers stored in a digital oscillator that govern what sort of waveshape it generates.

Wavetable lookup - The process of accessing and putting out the numbers in a wavetable in some specified order.

Wa-wa - The sound created by the regular boost and cut of treble frequencies. Also, a signal processor unit, generally operated by a foot pedal.

Wheel - A controller used for pitch-bending or modulation.

White noise - A randon electronic noise signal (static) containing all audible frequencies. White noise can be filtered and modulated for composition purposes. *See* **Noise, white.**

White noise generator - *See* **Random generator.**

Winchester disk - In computers, a hard disk-drive capable of storing 30 megabytes on 30 tracks which is intended to overcome the speed and storage limitations of the floppy disk. It is called the Winchester due to the "30-30" designation.

Window - A separate viewing area on a video screen which allows you to see something besides the main display. Also, a music-only passage, in a commercial, to which a voice-over can be added.

Wire wrap - A way of making electrical connections without soldering. A special tool wraps the wire tightly around a square post and the sharp edges bite into the wire, producing a reliable connection.

Word - The fixed number of bits which most computers can handle at a time. Larger scientific and business computers usually have words 32 or more bits long, while minicomputers typically have 12- or 16-bit word lengths.

Working volts DC - The maximum operational voltage of a capacitor.

WORM drive - Write Once, Read Many. An optical storage device.

Wrap - The length of the tape's path along which tape and head are in intimate physical contact, in recording. *See* **Head alignment.** Also, in film, the days shooting is completed.

Write - When a disk drive records data on a disk, the computer is said to be "writing" information. To transfer data from the computer to a peripheral, usually the disk drive. Also, record (write head = record head).

Write-protect - To guard a floppy disk from being written to or changed so that data already on it cannot be destroyed. You write-protect a disk by affixing a small adhesive tab over the write-protect notch on the upper-right side of a floppy disk. Never write-protect current data disks.

Write-protect notch - The small square cutout in one edge of the disk's jacket which is sensed by the DOS before it permits data to be written to the disk itself.

Write-protect tab - A small adhesive sticker used to cover the write-protect notch on a disk.

WVDC - *See* **Working volts DC.**

Xx

XLR connector - Designed by Cannon, a connector used in professional studios for balanced line connection.

X-Modem - Invented by Ward Christansen, a communications protocol for modems which transfers data and checks for transmission errors, etc.

Yy

Y-cord - A cord with two male and one female, or two female and one male connectors.

Zz

Zenith - The rotation of a tape head around an axis. Also, tangency.

Zero crossing - A point at which a digitally encoded waveform or sample crosses the center value in the range of possible values.

ZIF - Zero Insertion Force.

Zipper noise - Low-level audio glitches caused when sweeping a digitally-controlled circuit over a quantized range of values.

Zone - A contiguous range of keys on a keyboard.

CHRONOLOGY
OF SOME OF THE EVENTS SHAPING THE
CREATION, PRODUCTION, AND DISSEMINATION
OF
MUSIC IN THE 21st CENTURY

*1600 - DE MAGNETE. William Gilbert of Colchester initiated a scientific approach to the study of electrics.

1640's

*1640 - THE BAY PSALM BOOK. First book published in America.

*1646 - PSEUDODOXIA EPIDEMICA. Thomas Browne's treatise on electricity and magnetism.

1660's

*1663 - FRICTION MACHINE. Otto von Guericke in Magdeburg constructed the first friction machine for generating static electricity.

1740's

*1746 - LEYDEN JAR. The earliest form of capacitor developed by Pieter van Musschenbroek In Leyden, England.

1750's

*1753 - DENIS D'OR. An early electric music instrument invented by Divis.

*1759 - CLAVECIN ELECTRIQUE. An early electric music instrument, in which static electricity was used as part of the basic mechanism, invented by La Borde.

1770'S

*1770 - WILLIAM BILLINGS. The first native-born American composer to be published.

1790's

*1799 - VOLTAIC PILE. The first storage battery invented by Alessandro Volta.

1820's

*1820 - ELECTROMAGNETISM. The discovery by Hans Christian Oersted of the relationship between electricity and magnetism.

*1825 - ELECTROMAGNET. Construction of the first electromagnet by William Sturgeon at Woolwich, England.

1830's

*1830 - ELECTRIC TRANSFORMER. The first electrical transformers are produced by Michael Faraday in London, England.

*1831 - ELECTRIC MOTOR. The first electric motors are produced by Joseph Henry in Albany, New York.

*1837 - ELECTRIC BELL. Charles Grafton Page discovered the basic principle of the electric bell in Salem, Massachusetts.

*1838 - ROTATING TONE-WHEEL. Charles Delezenne of Lille, England constructed the first rotating tone-wheel.

1840's

*1848 - ELECTRICAL COMMUNICATIONS. Inventions of electrical telegraphy and Morse Code.

1850's

*1856 - ELECTRIC HARMONICA. Petrina of Prague built an electric harmonica based on four differently tuned Wagner hammers operated by keys.

1860's

*1860 - ELECTRICAL TELEPHONE. Capable only of limited intelligibility, Philipp Reis in Friedrichsdorf, Germany constructed the first electrical telephone.

*1864 - ELECTROMAGNETISM. The basic theory of electromagnetism is set forth by the British scientist, James C. Maxwell.

*1865 - BALDWIN COMPANY. Founded in Cincinnati, Ohio, by Dwight Hamilton Baldwin.

*1867 - ELECTROMECHANICAL PIANO. A player piano developed by Matthaus Hipp of Neuchate.

*1868 - ELECTRIC ACTION. The first successful organs with electric action were built by Albert Pechard and Charles Spackman Barker in France.

1870's

*1871 - TELEGRAPH. A Musical Telegraph Company founded by Elisha Gray in Rochester, New York.

*1875 - TELEPHONE. The first successful telephone invented by Alexander Graham Bell in the U.S.

*1876 - ELECTROMAGNETIC ORCHESTRA. An electric action orchestrion presented by Schmoele Brothers of Philadelphia, Pennsylvania.

*1876 - MUSICAL TELEGRAPH. An electromagnetic keyboard instrument developed by Elisha Gray in Chicago, Illinois. The MUSICAL TELEGRAPH included the earliest known use of a loudspeaker.

*1877 - CRISTALLOPHONE ELECTRIQUE. A player piano designed by Dieppe.

*1877 - CYLINDER PHONOGRAPH. The first cylinder phonograph is invented by Thomas A. Edison.

*1878 - PHONIC WHEEL. Lord Rayleigh incorporated a device for measuring the frequency of a tuning-fork.

*1879 - ELECTRICITY. Thomas A. Edison produces dynamos, generators, switches, and sockets.

1880's

*1881 - THEATROPHONE. A system of personal loudspeakers employed in the Paris Opera by Clement Ader.

*1882 - LIGHT BULB. Thomas A. Edison produces the first electric light bulb and lights up New York City.

*1883 - LAMP. Thomas A. Edison produces the EDISON EFFECT LAMP.

*1884 - ELECTROMAGNETS. Robert Kirk Boyle of Liverpool, England developed a system in which strings mounted on a frame and soundboard were activated by electromagnets; the first patent for a specifically musical application of electricity to produce sustained sounds.

*1884 - ELEKTRISCHES MUSIKINSTRUMENT. One of the first music instruments to use telephone earpieces as loudspeakers.

*1885 - ELEKTROPHONISCHES KLAVIER. Richard Eisenmann of Berlin, Germany used electromagnets to activate piano strings.

*1886 - POLYPHON. Various mechanical instruments manufactured by Polyhphon Musikwerke In Leipzig, Germany.

*1887 - YAMAHA. Manufacturers of a variety of products including acoustic instruments, electronic pianos, organs, and guitars, monophonic and polyphonic synthesizers, etc., the firm was founded by Torakusu Yamaha in Hamamatsu, Japan.

*1888 - PHOTOELECTRIC TONE-WHEEL. Ernest Mercadier in France introduced a photoelectric tone-wheel system for multiplex telegraphy.

1890's

*1890 - WURLITZER. Manufacturers of acoustic instruments, electronic pianos and organs, etc., The Rudolph Wurlitzer Company was founded by Franz Rudolph Wurlitzer in Cincinnati, Ohio. In 1957 the name was changed to the Wurlitzer Company.

*1891 - MOTION PICTURES. Thomas A. Edison sets up first motion picture studio, the BLACK MYRIYA.

*1892 - PLAYER PIANO. The player piano becomes popular creating a demand for player piano rolls.

*1893 - TELEFONHIRMONDO. A land-line broadcasting system initiated in Budapest, Hungary.

*1894 - PHONOGRAPH RECORD. The first commericial disk recordings appear in the U.S. market.

*1895 - PUBLISHING. Large music publishing firms are established in the U.S.

*1899 - SINGING ARC. A monophonic electronic instrument developed by William Du Bois Duddell in London, England.

* 1899 - TONOPHONE. An electrically powered, coin-operated Barrel piano by Wurlitzer.

1900's

*1900 - PUBLISHING. Music publishing grows; an estimated 100 songs sell a million copies each at a time when the U.S. population was about 90 million.

*1901 - TALKING MACHINE. The Victor Talking Machine Company is incorporated and develops 10,000 record dealers.

*1904 - OSCILLATION VALVE. A diode thermionic oscillation valve introduced by John Ambrose Fleming in London, England.

*1906 - AUXETOPHONE. An amplification system, powered by compressed air, developed by Charles Parson to enable conductor Henry Wood to amplify the orchestral double bass section.

*1906 - TELHARMONIUM. An electromechanical keyboard instrument invented by Thaddeus Cahill in Holyoke, Massachusetts.

*1907 - VALVE AMPLIFIER. The first valve amplifier is developed by Lee de Forest in New York.

*1909 - COPYRIGHT. The U.S. Congress passes the historic Copyright Law which provides published MECHANICAL RIGHTS in recorded music.

1910's

*1911 - ELECTRONIC OSCILLATOR. The first electronic oscillator is produced by W. Burstyn.

*1915 - AUDION PIANO. An electronic keyboard instrument developed by Lee de Forest, the first electronic instrument to exploit the vacuum tube.

*1916 - VIBRAPHONE. A metallophone of the bar percussion family developed by Hermann Winterhoff and manufactured by the Leedy Drum Company.

*1917 - JAZZ. The first jazz record is released.

*1917 - RADIO. Radio broadcasting for military purposes began.

*1919 - NEO-BECHSTEIN-FLUGEL. An electronic piano designed by Walther Nernst, H. Driescher, S. Franco, and Oskar Vierling and manufactured by Bechstein and Siemens & Halske in Berlin, Germany.

1920's

*1920 - ASCAP. The American Society of Composers, Authors and Publishers is established giving music publishers and writers income from performances of their music.

*1920 - RADIO. The first permanent radio station, KDKA is established in Pittsburgh.

*1921 - RECORDS. One-hundred million records are produced in the U.S.

*1922 - THIRING PIANO. An electronic keyboard instrument invented by Professor Thiring in Vienna, Austria.

*1922 - ETHEROPHONE. An electronic music instrument developed in Russia which was also called the THEREMINOVOX.

*1923 - RADIO. There are 500 radio stations licensed to broadcast. ATT inaugurates the first radio network.

*1924 - ELEKTROPHON. An electronic music instrument developed by Jorg Mager in Berlin, Germany.

*1924 - RECORDING. Bell Laboratories develops an electrical process for recording, increasing audible range over the earlier acoustical recordings to 100-5000 Hz.

*1924 - THEREMIN. A monophonic electronic instrument introduced at the Physico-Technical Institute in Petrograd, Russia and named for the Russian scientist/inventor Leon Theremin.

*1925 - ELECTRONIC AMPLIFIER. The first electronic amplifiers are developed.

*1925 - MIDGLEY-WALKER ORGAN. An electronic organ developed by A.H. Midgley and A.M. Midgley and manufactured in 1937 by J.W. Walker & Sons in Ruislip, Middlesex, England.

*1926 - ELECTRIFIED PIANO. A Chickering Ampico player piano was first electrified in Atlantic City, New Jersey.

*1926 - OMNITONIUM. An electronic instrument developed by Jorg Mager.

*1926 - PIANORAD. An electronic keyboard instrument constructed at the Radio News Laboratories by Clyde J. Fitch and designed by Hugo Gernsback.

*1926 - RADIANO. A piano microphone developed by Fred W. Roehm and Frank W. Adsit.

*1926 - SPHAROPHON. Monophonic electronic instruments invented by Jorg Mager and built by the Larenz Company in Berlin, Germany.

*1927 - CELLULOPHONE. A photoelectric keyboard instrument developed by Pierre Toulon and Krugg Bass in France.

*1927 - DYNAPHONE. A monophonic electronic instrument developed by Rene Bertrand in Paris, France.

*1927 - ELEKTRONISCHE ZAUBERGEIGE. A type of Theremin con-
structed by Erich Zitmann-Zirini in Berlin, Germany.

*1927 - KALEIDOPHON. An early electronic instrument built by Jorg
Mager in Germany.

*1927 - SUPERPIANO. An electric piano developed by Emmerich
Spielmann and constructed by Klavierfabrik Rudolf Stelzhammer in
Vienna, Austria.

*1928 - ELECTRONIC MONOCHORD. An electronic music instrument
developed from the Trautonium.

*1928 - ONDES MARTENOT. A monophonic electronic instrument in-
vented by Maurice Martenot in Paris, France.

*1928 - PIANO ELECTRIQUE. An electric piano developed by Joseph
Bethenod in Paris, France.

*1929 - ELECTRONDE. A type of battery-powered Theremin constructed
by Martin Taubmann in Berlin, Germany.

*1929 - RADIO. The meteoric rise of radio popularity slows down progress
in the recording industry. Stock market crash.

*1929 - SOUND FILM. Sound film is introduced in the U.S. and the USSR.

1930's

*1930 - EMICON. A monophonic electronic music instrument developed
by John Halmagyi and Nicholas Langer in the U.S.

*1930 - HELLERTION. A monophonic electronic instrument developed by Bruno Helberger, Peter Lertes, and Schneider-Opel in Frankfurt, Germany.

*1930 - ONDIUM PECHADRE. A monophonic electronic instrument developed by H.C.R. Pechadre in France.

*1930 - RADIOTONE. A monophonic electroacoustic keyboard instrument developed by Gabriel Boreau at the Societe d'Etudes et de Construction d'Instruments de Musique in Paris, France.

*1930 - SONAR. A monophonic electronic instrument designed by N. Ana'yev in Moscow, Russia.

*1930 - TRAUTONIUM. A monophonic electronic music instrument invented by Friedrich Trautwein in Berlin, Germany.

*1931 - ELEKTROAKUSTISCHE GRALSGLOCKEN. A set of electromagnetic Javanese gongs by Jorg Mager.

*1931 - HAWAIIAN STEEL GUITAR. The Rickenbacker Frying Pan, a small steel guitar, was designed. In 1934, the first leg-mounted electric steel guitars were manufactured by the Gibson Company.

*1931 - PARTITUROPHON. A monophonic electronic keyboard instrument built by Jorg Mager in Darmstadt, Germany.

*1931 - PIEZOELECTRIC AIR MICROPHONE. C.B.Sawyer devised the first successful version after attempts by Pierre and Jacques Curie and others beginning in 1883.

*1931 - RADIO ORGAN OF A TRILLION TONES. A photoelectric keyboard instrument developed by Arnold Lesti in Hollywood, California.

*1931 - RANGERTONE ORGAN. A two-manual electronic organ developed by Richard H. Ranger in Newark, New Jersey.

*1931 - RHYTHMICON. The first electronic percussion instrument, designed by Lev Termen.

*1932 - ELECTRIC PIANO. The first electric piano was developed by Benjamin F. Miessner in Milburn, New Jersey.

*1932 - EMIRITON. A monophonic electronic instrument developed by Dzerzhkovich, Ivanov, Kreytser, and Rimsky-Korsakov in Moscow, Russia at the Research Institute of the Musical Instrument Industry.

*1932 - GNOME. An electronic keyboard instrument developed by Ivan Eremeeff in Philadelphia, Pennsylvania.

*1932 - PIANO-HARP. A polyphonic electronic keyboard instrument built by Joseph Bethenod in Paris, France.

*1932 - VARIAPHONE. A photoelectric composition machine developed by Evgeny Aleksandrovich Sholpo in Leningrad, Russia.

*1933 - EKVODIN. A monophonic electronic instrument invented by Andrey Aleksandrovich Volodin and Konstantin Koval'sky in Moscow, Russia.

*1933 - LICHTTON-ORGEL. An electronic organ developed by Edwin Welte and W. Faass in Freiburg, Germany.

*1933 - MAGNETON. An electronic organ developed by Rudolf Steizhammer and W. Lenk in Vienna, Austria.

*1933 - MAKHONINE VIOLIN. An electric violin invented by Ivan Makhonin in France.

*1933 - POLYTONE. A photoelectric keyboard instrument developed by Arnold Lesti and Frederick M. Sammis at RCA in Hollywood, California.

*1933 - UNA-FON. An electronic organ manufactured by J.C. Deagan of Chicago, Illinois.

*1934 - ELECTRIC GUITAR. The first electric guitars were designed by Lloyd Loar at the Gibson Company and manufactured by Loar and Lewis A. Williams at the Acousti-Lectric Company.

*1934 - ELECTRONE. An electronic organ designed by Leslie Bourn and manufactured by the John Compton Organ Company.

*1934 - HAMMOND ORGAN. An electronic instrument invented by Laurens Hammond and John M. Hanert in 1934 in Chicago, Illinois.

*1934 - ORGATRON. An electronic organ invented by Frederick Albert Hoschke and manufactured by the Everett Piano Company in South Haven, Michigan.

*1934 - ORGUE RADIOSYNTHETIQUE. An electroacoustic pipe organ designed by Abbe Pujet and constructed by Cavaille-Colland in France.

*1934 - RADIO. The FCC is established by the Federal Communications Act. Remote wires are set up for live broadcasts of music.

*1934 - RHYTHMICON. An electronic music instrument designed by Henry Cowell and built by Leon Theremin.

*1934 - SYNTRONIC ORGAN. An electronic organ developed by Ivan Eremeeff at radio station WCAU in Philadelphia, Pennsylvania.

* 1934 - WAVE ORGAN. An electronic organ developed by Morse Robb and manufactured by the Robb Wave Organ Company in Belleville, Ontario, Canada.

*1935 - ETHONIUM. A Theremin-like instrument constructed by G.G. Blake in London, England.

* 1935 - MINIPIANO. An electric piano based on Benjamin F. Miessner's ELECTRONIC PIANO and manufactured by Hardman, Peck & Company, New York.

*1935 - PHOTONA. A photoelectric keyboard instrument developed by Ivan Eremeeff in Philadelphia, Pennsylvania.

*1935 - RECORD ALBUM. First record albums appear. Dealers sell record players near cost to encourage record sales.

*1936 - PIANOTRON. An electric piano manufactured by the Everett Piano Company of South Haven, Michigan.

*1936 - ELEKTROCHORD. An electric piano designed by Oskar Vierling and manufactured by August Forster Klavierfabrik in Lobau, Saxony.

*1936 - HELIOPHON. An electronic keyboard instrument developed by Bruno Helberger and Peter Lertes in Berlin, Germany.

*1936 - KRAFT DURCH FREUDE-GROSSTON-ORGEL. An electronic organ designed by Oskar Vierling at the Heinrich-Hertz-Institut fur-Schwingungsforschung in Berlin, Germany commissioned for use at the 1936 Olympic Games.

*1936 - RESONOSCOPE. An electrical pitch-carrying instrument introduced in the U.S.

*1936 - SINGING KEYBOARD. An electro-mechanical keyboard designed by Frederick M. Sammis at RCA in Hollywood, California.

*1936 - VOCODER. An electronic-music device developed by Homer Dudley at the Bell Telephone Laboratories in Murray Hill, New Jersey.

*1937 - CHORUS GENERATOR. First introduced by the Hammond Organ Company.

*1937 - ELECTONE. An electric piano designed by Maurice K. Bretzfelder and Manufactured by Krakauer Brothers of New York.

*1937 - OSCILLION. A monophonic electronic instrument designed by William E. Danforth at the Franklin Institute in Philadelphia, Pennsylvania.

*1937 - VARIACHORD. An electronic piano developed by Dr. Pollak-Rudin in Vienna, Austria.

*1937 - VODER. A keyboard-operated speaking machine developed by Homer Dudley at the Bell Telephone Laboratories in Murray Hill, New Jersey.

*1938 - CHROMATIC ELECTRONIC TIMPANI. Built by Benjamin F. Miessner.

*1938 - MELODIUM. A monophonic electronic keyboard instrument developed by Harold Bode and Oskar Vierling in Berlin, Germany.

*1938 - PIANOTRON. A portable electric piano manufactured by Selmer in London, England.

*1938 - THIENHAUS-CEMBALO. An electric harpsichord developed by Erich Thienhaus at the Physikalisch-Technische Reichsanstalt in Berlin, Germany.

*1938 - TOURNIER ORGAN. An electronic organ developed by Marcel Tournier in Paris, France.

*1938- WARBO FORMANT-ORGEL. A partially polyphonic instrument introduced by Harald Bode.

*1939 - AMERICAN ALLEN ORGAN. The first fully electronic organ to be marketed.

*1939 - BMI. Broadcast Music Incorporated is established by the National Association of Broadcasters.

*1939 - NOVACHORD. An electronic music instrument developed by Laurens Hammond and C.N. Williams and manufactured by the Hammond Organ Company.

*1939 - STANDARD PITCH. A1 = 440 vibrations per second was unanimously adopted as the standard pitch by the International Conference on Pitch held in London, England.

*1939 - STORYTONE. An upright electric piano designed by engineers at RCA and manufactured by the Story and Clark Piano Company of New York.

*1939 - JUKE BOX. Juke box operators were buying 13 million records annually to serve their machines.

1940's

*1940 - LESLIE SPEAKER. A speaker system which included separate rotating low and high frequency speakers designed by Donald J. Leslie and manufactured by the Electro-Music Company in Pasadena, California.

*1940 - SOLOVOX. A monophonic electronic music instrument designed by Laurens Hammond, Thomas J. George, and John M. Hanert and manufactured by the Hammond Organ Company in Chicago, Illinois.

*1941 - ONDIOLINE. A monophonic piano attachment developed by Georges Jenny and manufactured by Les Ondes Georges Jenny (La Musique Electronique) in Paris, France.

*1941 - RADIO. The FCC authorizes the first commercial FM stations.

*1941 - SONOVOX. A sound-effects device developed by Gilbert M. Wright and manufactured by Wright-Sonovox in Los Angeles, California.

*1942 - AF of M. The American Federation of Musicians strike (1942-1945) against record companies paralyzes the industry.

*1942 - ENIAC (Electronic Numerical Integrator and Computer). The first electronic digital computer was built at the University of Pennsylvania.

*1943 - RECORDER. The first wire recorder is developed in Germany.

*1944 - ELECTRONIC MUSIC BOX. A predecessor of the RCA ELECTRONIC MUSIC SYNTHESIZER developed by Earle Lewis Kent at the C.G. Conn Corporation in Elkhart, Indiana.

*1944 - FENDER. Leo Fender and Clayton Orr Kauffman establish the K & F Company to produce electric steel guitars. In 1946 Fender founded the Fender Electric Company.

*1945 - HANERT ELECTRICAL ORCHESTRA. A graphic composition machine developed by John Marshall Hanert at the Hammond Organ Company in Chicago, Illinois.

*1945 - RADIO. 950 AM stations are on the air at the end of World War II.

*1946 - ELECTRONIC SACBUT. A monophonic electronic music instrument developed by Hugh Le Caine in Ottawa, Canada.

*1946 - RADIO. Rapid growth of radio with 500 additional AM and FM stations.

*1947 -BALDWIN ORGAN. An electronic organ, designed by Winston E. Kock, manufactured by the Baldwin Piano and Organ Company.

*1947 - CONNSONATA. An electronic organ designed by Earle L. Kent and manufactured by C.G. Conn in Elkhart, Indiana.

*1947 - MELOCHORD. A monophonic electronic keyboard instrument developed by Harald Bode in Neubeuern, Germany and constructed by the Haberlein Company.

*1947 - TRANSISTOR. William Bradford Shockley invents the transistor at Bell Telephone Laboratories.

*1948 - COMPOSERTRON. An electronic composition machine developed by Osmond Kendall at the National Research Council of Canada in Ottawa.

*1948 - ELECTRONIUM. A monophonic electronic keyboard instrument developed by Rene Seybold and manufactured by Hohner in Trossingen, Germany.

*1948 - FRENCH NATIONAL RADIO - Site of the first organized experimental work in MUSIQUE CONCRETE.

*1948 - LP. The long-playing microgroove phonograph record was introduced by Columbia.

*1948 - MILLER ORGAN. An electronic organ designed by Constant Martin and manufactured by the Stanley L. Miller Organ Company.

*1948 - THOMAS ORGAN. An electronic organ manufactured by the Thomas Organ Company at North Hollywood and Sepulveda, California.

*1949 - ELECTRONIC CARILLON. The first electronic carillon was devised by Constant Martin.

*1949 - LOWREY ORGAN. An electronic organ manufactured by the Lowrey Organ Company in Lincolnwood, Illinois.

*1949 - MIXTUR-TRAUTONIUM. A monophonic electronic instrument developed by Oskar Sala in Berlin, Germany.

*1949 - TELEVISION. The increasing popularity of television greatly reduces radio advertising revenues and record sales.

1950's

*1950 - MINSHALL ORGAN. An electronic organ designed by George Hadden and manufactured by Minshall Organ of Brattleboro, Vermont.

*1950 - RADAREED ORGAN. An electronic organ designed by George Gubbins in the U.S.

*1950 - VIERLING ORGAN. An electronic organ developed by Oskar Vierling and manufactured by Ebermannstadt in Nuremberg, Germany.

*1950 - WOBBLE ORGAN. A monophonic electronic instrument developed by L.A. Meacham in the U.S.

*1951 - AWB ORGAN. An electronic organ, designed by Harald Bode and Heinz Ahlborn and manufactured by Apparatewerk Bayern in Dachau, Germany.

*1951 - DIGITAL COMPUTER. First marketed commercially by Remington Rand in the U.S.

*1951 - PIANETTA. A monophonic piano attachment manufactured by Richard Lipp & Sohn.

*1951 - POLYCHORD III. An electronic organ developed by Harald Bode and manufactured by Apparatewerk Bayern in Dachau, Germany.

*1951 - RADIO COLOGNE. The first major electronic music studio was established by Dr. Herbert Eimert, Cologne, Germany.

*1951 - THYRATONE. A monophonic three-octave piano attachment developed by Richard H. Dorf and manufactured by the General Electric Company in New York.

*1952 - COLUMBIA-PRINCETON ELECTRONIC MUSIC CENTER. Founded by Otto Luening and Vladimir Ussachevsky, the first electronic music studio to be established in the U.S.

*1952 - DEREUX ORGAN. An electronic organ developed by Jean-Adolphe Dereux in Paris, France.

*1952 - UNIVOX. A monophonic piano attachment developed by Leslie James Hills and manufactured by Jennings Musical Instruments of Dartford, Kent, England.

*1953 - ELEKTRONISCHE MONOCHORD. A monophonic two-manual electronic instrument developed by Friedrich Trautwein for the Nordwestdeutscher Rundfunk in the Cologne, Germany electronic music studio.

*1953 - TELEVISION. The rapid growth of television greatly impacts network radio eliminating most live music and radio staff orchestras. Electrical transcriptions and disk jockeys begin to dominate radio.

* 1953 - TUTTIVOX. An electronic organ developed by Harald Bode and manufactured by Jorgensen Electronic in Dusseldorf, Germany.

*1954 - CLAVIER. An electronic piano developed by Lloyd Loar and manufactured by the Acousti-Lectric Company in Kalamazoo, Michigan.

*1954 - HOHNERVOX. An electronic keyboard instrument developed and manufactured by Hohner in Trossingen, Germany.

*1954 - PIANOPHON. An electric piano manufactured by Beleton of Berlin, Germany.

*1955 - ELECTRONIC TONE GENERATOR. Introduced by the Allen Organ Company.

*1955 - GULBRANSEN ORGAN. An electronic organ manufactured by the Gulbransen Company in Melrose Park, Illinois.

*1955 - ILLIAC COMPUTER. A computer used in music composition by Professors Issacson and Hiller at the University of Illinois.

*1955 - RCA ELECTRONIC MUSIC SYNTHESIZER. An electronic composition machine developed by Harry F. Olson and Herbert F. Belar and produced by the Radio Corporation of America in Princeton, New Jersey.

*1955 - RECORDS. Phonograph record clubs are begun by Columbia, followed by RCA and Capitol.

*1955 - TOCCATA ORGAN. An electronic organ designed by Ernst Schreiber and manufactured by the Werk fur Fernsehelektronik in Germany.

*1956 - ANS. A photoelectric composition machine developed by Evgeny Murzin.

*1957 - COMPUTER SOUND SYNTHESIS. First experiments carried out by Max Mathews at the Bell Telephone Laboratories, Murray Hill, New Jersey.

* 1957 - INTEGRATED CIRCUIT. The first IC was crafted by Jack Kilby at Texas Instruments.

* 1957 - KINSMAN ORGAN. An electronic organ developed by Richard H. Dorf and colleagues at the Minshall Organ Company and manufactured by the Kinsman Manufacturing Company in Laconia, New Hampshire.

*1957 - RECORDS. Rack jobbing begins.

*1957 - SIEMENS SYNTHESIZER. An electronic compositon machine designed by Jelmut Klein and W. Schaaf and developed at Siemens & Halske in Munich, Germany for the Studio fur Elektronische Musik.

*1958 - ELECTONE. An electronic organ manufactured by Yamaha, Nippon Gakki CompanyIn Hamamatsu, Japan.

*1958 - RECORDS. Stereo is introduced in commercial phonograph records.

*1958 - RODGERS ORGAN. An electronic organ manufactured by the Rodgers Organ Company in Hillsboro, Oregon.

*1959 - RECORDS. Classical music's first million-seller: Van Cliburn's performance of Tchaikovsky's CONCERTO FOR PIANO AND ORCHESTRA.

1960's

*1960 - CLAVINET. An electronic keyboard instrument manufactured by Hohner in Trossingen, Germany.

*1960 - KRISTADIN. An electronic organ constructed at the Sound Recording Institute in Moscow, Russia.

*1960 - SIDE MAN. An electronic percussion instrument manufactured by Wurlitzer.

*1961 - MUSIKMASKIN I. A sound sculpture constructed by Knut Wiggen, Per-Olof Stromberg, and Oyvind Fahlstrom in Stockholm, Sweden.

*1961 - YUNOST'. An electronic organ built at the Murov Radio Works in Russia.

*1961 - RADIO. The FCC authorizes multiplex broadcasting. FM stations greatly increase in number.

*1962 - DIRECT SYNTHESIS. Max Mathews completed first definitive program known as MUSIC4.

*1962 - PIANET. An electric piano designed by Richard Bierl and Ernst Zacharias and manufactured by Hohner in Trossingen, Germany.

*1962 - RECORDS. Formation of NARM by record wholesalers.

*1962 - SNOBOL. A computer programming language developed at the Bell Laboratories.

*1962 - SUBHARCHORD. A monophonic electronic instrument developed by Ernst Schreiber at Rundfunk und Fernsehtechnisches Zentralamt der Deutschen Post in Berlin, Germany.

*1963 - ELECTROMAGNETIC MUSICAL. A series of amplified sound sculptures constructed by Taki.

*1963 - GUITARET. An electromagnetically amplified lamellaphone manufactured in Trossingen, Germany. by Hohner.

*1963 - MUSICOMP (MUSIC SIMULATOR-INTERPRETER FOR COMPOSITION PROCEDURES). A computer program developed by Professors Baker and Hiller at the University Of Illinois.

*1964 - BUCHLA SYNTHESIZER. First synthesizer designed by Donald F. Buchla and manufactured by Buchla & Associates, Berkeley, California.

*1964 - ELKA ORGAN. An electronic organ designed by S. Fideli, G. Mazzini, and Orlandoni and manufactured by the Elka Company in Castelfidardo.

*1964 - ELEKTRONMUSIKSTUDION (EMS). Established by Swedish Radio, Gunar Hellstrom and Knut Wiggen set up the first electronic music studio which, by 1970, became the first fully computer-controlled electronic music studio in the world.

*1964 - MELLOTRON. An electromechanical keyboard instrument developed by Frank Leslie and Norman Bradley and manufactured by the Mellotron Manufacturing Company.

*1964 - MOOG. A synthesizer manufacturing company founded by Robert A. Moog in Trumansburg, New York. Moog marketed the world's first commercial synthesizer and developed the MINIMOOG, SONIC SIX, SATELLITE, MICROMOOG, POLYMOOG, and others.

*1964 - PHILICORDA. An electronic organ manufactured by Philips Electrical in Croydon, England and Philips Gloeilampfabrieken in Eindhoven, Germany.

*1964 - VOLTAGE-CONTROLLED SYNTHESIZER. Developed by Robert A. Moog.

*1965 - MUSICAL INFORMATION RETRIEVAL (MIR). A computer program for the theoretical analysis and cataloging of existing music compositions developed by Professors Lockwood and Mendel at Princeton University.

*1965 - ORAMICS. A photoelectric composition machine developed by Daphne Oram in Fairseat, Kent, England.

*1965 - RHODES ELECTRIC PIANO. An electric piano designed by Harold Rhodes and manufactured by Rhodes Keyboard Instruments in Santa Ana and Fullerton, California.

*1965 - TRANSICORD. An electronic piano accordian manufactured by Farfisa of Ancona.

*1966 - WYVERN ORGAN. An electronic organ designed by Kenneth Burge and Tony Korlander and manufactured by Wyvern Church Organs in Bideford, Devon, England.

*1967 - DIGITAL ORGAN. Ralph Deutsch filed the first patent in the U.S for a digital organ.

*1967 - JOHANNUS ORGAN. An electronic organ developed by Johannus Versteegt and manufactured by Johannus Orgelbouw in Ede (Arnhem).

*1968 - KORG. Electronic instruments, e.g., the Korg synthesizer, the

Polysix, Delta, Lambda, Trident and various electronic pianos, string synthesizers, electronic percussion units, guitar synthesizers, etc., manufactured by the Keio Electronic Laboratory Corporation in Tokyo, Japan.

*1968 - STRING SYNTHESIZER. A keyboard synthesizer, which electronically imitates the sound of a string ensemble, developed as a portable substitute for the MELLOTRON.

*1968 - STYLOPHONE. A small monophonic electronic keyboard instrument developed by Brian Jarvis and manufactured by Dubreq in London, England.

*1969 - ELECTRONIC MUSIC STUDIOS (EMS). A company of synthesizer and electronic instrument manufacturers founded in Putney, London, England by Peter Zinovieff.

*1969 - FRAP (FLAT RESPONSE AUDIO PICKUP). A special contact microphone developed by Arnie Lazarus.

*1969 - KRAAKDOOS. A synthesizer designed by Michel Waisvisz and Geert Hamelberg in the Hague.

*1969 - PUTNEY SYNTHESIZER. A music synthesizer developed by Don Banks.

*1969 - RAHNMENHARFE. An amplified string instrument constructed by Mauricio Kagel.

*1969 - RECORD. Release of the historic recording with voltage-controlled equipment by Walter Carlos, SWITCHED ON BACH.

1970's

*1970 - CHAPMAN STICK. A 10-string electric music instrument invented by Emmet Chapman.

*1970 - GROOVE (GENERATED REAL-TIME OPERATIONS ON VOLTAGE-CONTROLLED EQUIPMENT). Max Mathews completed one of the first hybrid systems at the Bell Telephone Laboratories.

*1970 - MAKIN ORGAN. An electronic organ manufactured by Compton-Makin in Rochdale, Lancashire, England.

*1970 - MINIMOOG. A monophonic synthesizer designed by Robert A. Moog, William Hemsath, Chad Hunt, and James Scott and manufactured by the R.A. Moog Company in Trumansburg, New York.

*1970 - PIANOMATE. A keyless electronic organ manufactured in London, England.

*1970 - SAL-MAR CONSTRUCTION. A hybrid digital-analog electronic instrument developed by Salvatore Martirano and Sergio Franco at the University of Illinois.

*1971 - DIGITAL COMPUTER ORGAN. An organ manufactured by Allen.

*1971 - GAME (GENERATEUR AUTOMATIQUE DE MUSIQUE ELECTRONIIQUE). A composition machine developed by Leo Kupper in Belgium.

*1971 - ODYSSEY. A monophonic synthesizer manufactured by Arp Instruments.

*1971 - TOCCATA ORGAN. An electronic organ manufactured by Crumar in Germany.

*1972 - ELECTROCOMP SYNTHESIZER. A portable electronic Music synthesizer developed by Dale Blake, Fred Locke, Norm Milliard, and Jeff Murray and manufactured by Electronic Music Labs in Talcottville, Connecticut.

*1972 - E-MU SYSTEMS. A synthesizer/electronic instruments manufacturer is established in Santa Clara, California.

*1972 - 4004 - The first well-publicized true microprocessor developed by Intel.

*1972 - RECORDS. Use of 16 and 24-track recording consoles.

*1972 - ROLAND. A Japanese company of electronic instrument manufacturers, founded in Osaka, Japan by electronics designer Ikutaro Kakehashi.

*1972 - SCALATRON. An electronic keyboard instrument developed by George Secor and Hermann Pedtke and manufactured by Motorola in Chicago, Illinois.

*1972 - SCORE. A special interpreting software program developed by Leland Smith at Stanford University.

*1972 - SYNCLAVIER. A polyphonic digital synthesizer developed by Sydney Alonso, Cameron Jones, and Jon Appleton and manufactured by the New England Digital Corporation of White River Junction, Vermont.

*1972 - VOCOM. The earliest design for a mixed digital sytem produced by Zinovieff.

*1973 - DARTMOUTH DIGITAL SYNTHESIZER. Developed by Sydney, Jon Appleton, and Cameron Jones at Dartmouth College.

*1973 - GMEBOGOSSE. A portable synthesizer system designed for young children by Christian Clozier, Jean-Claude Le Duc and Pierre Boeswillwald in France and constructed at the Groupe de Musique Experimentals de Bourges.

*1973 - KALEIDOPHON. A synthesizer controller developed by David Vorhaus in London, England.

*1973 - QASAR. A digital synthesizer designed by Anthony Furse and manufactured by Creative Strategies in Sydney, Australia.

*1974 - OBERHEIM. A range of synthesizers designed by Tom Oberheim and manufactured by Oberheim Electronics in Santa Monica and Los Angeles, California. They include the SYNTHESIZER EXPANDER MODULE, OB-1, OB-X, OBXA, OB-SX, OB-XPANDER, DSX, DMX and the DX.

*1974 PAIA. Synthesizers, including the GNOME microsynthesizer and the monophonic programmable PROTEUS, designed by Johns S. Simonton and manufactured by PAIA Electronics in Oklahoma City, Oklahoma.

*1974 - SERGE. A modular synthesizer designed by Serge Tcherepnin and manufactured by Serge Modular Music Systems in Hollywood and San Francisco, California.

*1975 - BICROTRON. An electromechanical keyboard instrument designed by Dave Biro and Rick Wakeman and manufactured by Birotronics in Buckinghamshire, England.

*1975 - CASIO COMPUTER COMPANY. Founded by Mr. Kashio in Tokyo, Japan.

*1975. GNOME - A small synthesizer manufactured by Paia Electronics in 1975 in Oklahoma City, Oklahoma.

*1975 - LYRICON. An electronic wind instrument that controls a synthesizer developed by Bill Bernardi and Roger Noble and manufactured by Computone, Inc. in Hanover, Massachusetts.

*1975 - NORWICH ORGAN. An electronic organ manufactured by Norwich Organ Manufacturers.

*1976 - COPYRIGHT. The U.S. Congress passes the 1976 statute which preempts nearly all other copyright laws, federal, state and Common Law.

*1976 - RADIO. There were 4,497 commercial AM stations; 2,873 commercial FM stations; 870 non-commercial FM stations; 8,240 total stations in operation with radio revenues of $1.8 billion And TV revenues of $4.2 billion.

*1977 - DMX-1000. A polyphonic digital synthesizer developed by Dean Wallraff and manufactured by Digital Music Systems in Boston, Massachusetts.

*1977 - GUITAR SYNTHESIZER. The first true guitar synthesizer was introduced by Roland.

*1977 - RECORDING. Sophistication of technology increases including use of synthesizers, computer-assisted mixing, digital recording.

*1977 - SSSP (STRUCTURED SOUND SYNTHESIS PROJECT). A polyphonic digital synthesizer developed by William Buxton at the University of Toronto in Canada. Added later were the SSSP COMPOSITION SYSTEM, SSSP CONDUCT SYSTEM, and the SSSP TOUCH-SENSITIVE DRUM.

*1977 - SYNARE. Electronic percussion instruments manufactured by Star Instruments of Stafford Springs, Connecticutt.

*1978 - DIMI. A digital synthesizer developed by Erkki Kurenniemi and Jukka Ruohamaki and manufactured by Digelius Electronics in Helsinki, Finland.

*1978 - PIANOCORDER. An electronic system introduced by the Superscope Company of Morgantown, North Carolina.

*1978 - PPP WAVE COMPUTER. A polyphonic digital synthesizer developed by Wolfgang Palm and manufactured by Palm Production Germany in Hamburg, Germany. They also manufactured the PPG PROGRAMMABLE SYNTHESIZER, SYSTEM 340, WAVE COMPUTER, EVENT GENERATOR, and the WAVETERM.

*1978 - PROPHET. A synthesizer developed by Dave Smith and manufactured by Sequential Circuits in San Jose, California. They also manufactured PROPHET 10, PRO-ONE, PROPHET 600, and the REMOTE PROPHET.

*1978 - RECORDS. Record business increases rapidly with multinational conglomerates forming and 5,000 industry leaders from 52 countries attending the international music conference.

*1978 - SYNDRUM. An electronic percussion instrument invented by Joe Pollard and manufactured by Syndrum of South El Monte, California.

*1978 - WASP. A synthesizer developed by Adrian Wagner and Chris Huggett and manufactured by Electronic Dream Plant in Combe, England.

*1979 - CON BRIO. A polyphonic digital synthesizer developed by Danziger, Lieberman and Ryan and manufactured by Con Brio Electronics of Pasadena, California.

*1979 - ELECTRONIC VALVE INSTRUMENT. An electronic wind instrument that controls a synthesizer developed by Nyle A. Steiner and manufactured by Steiner-Parker in Salt Lake City, Utah.

*1979 - FAIRLIGHT. A polyphonic digital synthesizer designed by Peter Vogel and Kim Ryrie and manufactured by Fairlight Instruments in Sydney, Australia.

*1979 - IMPACT. A hybrid system written by Michael Hinton.

1980's

*1980 - CASIOTONE. A small electronic organ manufactured by the Casio Computer Company in Tokyo, Japan.

*1980 - C-DUCER. A special contact microphone designed by John Ribet, Francis Townsend, and Andre Walton and made by C-Tape Developments of Alton, Hampshire, England.

*1980 - THE KIT. An electronic percussion instrument developed by Clive Button and manufactured in Willingham, Cambridgeshire, England by MPC Electronics.

*1980 - CHROMA. A synthesizer designed by Philip Dodds and manufactured by Rhodes Keyboard Instruments in Fullerton, California.

*1980 - LINN DRUM. An electronic percussion instrument developed by Roger Linn and Roger Moffatt and manufactured by Linn Electronics in Hollywood and Tarzana, California.

*1980 - POLYSIX. A programmable polyphonic Korbsynthesizer manfactured by Keio in Tokyo, Japan.

*1980 - SIMMONS ELECTRONIC DRUMS. Electronic percussion in struments developed by Dave Simmons and manufactured by Simmons Electronics of St. Albans, Hertfordshire, England.

*1980 - TOUCHE. A synthesizer manufactured by Buchla.

*1981 - EMULATOR. An electronic keyboard instrument designed by Dave Rossum and manufactured by E-mu Systems in Santa Cruz, California.

*1981 - GENERAL DEVELOPMENT SYSTEM (GDS). A polyphonic digital synthesizer manufactured by the Digital Keyboards Division of Music Technology at Garden City Park, New York.

*1981 - OMNICHORD. An electronic instrument manufactured by Suzuki in Hamamatsu, Japan.

*1981 - SOUNDCHASER. A polyphonic digital synthesizer manufactured by Passport Designs of Half Moon Bay, California.

* 1981 - MTV (MUSIC TELEVISION). A promotional vehicle for the sale of records.

*1981 - OMNICHORD. An electronic instrument manufactured by Suzuki struments developed by Dave Simmons and manufactured by Simmons Electronics of St. Albans, Hertfordshire, England.

*1982 - SYNERGY. A polyphonic digital syhnthesizer designed by S. Jerrold Kaplan and manufactured by the Digital Keyboards division of Music Technology in Garden City Park, New York.

*1982 - SYNSONICS DRUMS. An electronic percussion instrument marketed by Mattel Electronics of California.

*1983 - DRUMULATOR. An electronic percussion unit manufactured by E-mu Systems.

*1985 - 4X. A polyphonic digital synthesizer developed by Giuiseppe di Giugno and manufactured by Sogitec in Boulogne, France.

TODAY

The proliferation of inventions and manufacturing of hardware and software since the mid-eighties has been staggering. The quality and longevity of this equipment will need to be evaluated at a future time by other authors. MIDI(Musical Instrument Digital Interface) has provided the major impetus for musicians in this period and is changing, expanding, and adapting to new music needs on a daily basis.

Following is a list of MIDI and MIDI-related hardware that is currently available.

SYNCHRONIZABLE TAPE SYSTEMS

*SYNCHRONOUS TECHNOLOGIE SMPL System, Chase-Lock

* FOSTEX   4050, A-8 (modified), B-16

*TASCAM   42, 48, 52, 58, MS-16

*OTARI   MS-70

MIDI CONTROL SYSTEMS

*IBANEZ   MIUB interface unit, IFC 60
                          Intelligent foot controller,
                          EPP400

*DYNACORD   MCCI Control Computer

*ROLAND   SBX-80

*VOYCE   LX-4

MIDI HARDWARE

*ROLAND   MPU-401, MUP-101, LPK-1,
                          STK-1, MPU 103, MPU 104
                          and 105, MD-8, MM-4, OP-
                          8M, MKS-900

*FORTE   MIDI-mod

*IBANEZ	MIU8
*TOA	D-4
*ASSIMILATION	MIDI Conductor
*AKAI	ME-15F
*YAMAHA	YMC10
*JL COOPER ELECTRONICS	MIDI Disk, MIDI switch box 16/20 effects switcher
*YAMAHA	YME8
*GARFIELD ELECTRONICS	MINI DOC, Doctor Click 2, Master Beat, Multi Trigger, Drum Doctor, Nano Doc, MIDI adaptor, FSK adaptor
*KORG	Compu-Dump, KMT-60, KMS-30, MEX-8000, DYP-1
*DECILLIONIX	MIDI-Madness
*OPCODE SYSTEMS	MIDIMAC
*SYNTECH	S-14, S-28, S-81
*WERSI	MIDI interface
*HYBRID ARTS	MIDIMATE
*OCTAVE PLATEAU	OP4001

*MUSIC DATA	MIDI interface
*PASSPORT	MIDI interface
	MIDI Pro interface
*MOOG	Song Producer
*SIMMONS	MTM
*LEMI	MIDI devices
*KAMLET ELECTRONICS	MIDI patcher

MIDI AMPLIFIERS

*PEAVEY	Programax 10, RMC TBA 2000
*DYNACORD	Reference Series

MIDI DIGITAL DELAYS AND REVERBS

*YAMAHA	REV7, D-1500
*PEAVEY	4000
*ROLAND	SRV 2000, SDE 2500
*LEXICON	PCM 70
*DYNACORD	PDD 14, DRP 16 (M), Bank B
*AKAI	ME 10D
*ART	DRI

*IBANEZ	DUE 4000, EP[P 400
*KORG	SDD 2000

MIDI SEQUENCERS

*ROLAND	MC-500, MSQ 100, MSQ 700
*YAMAHA	QXI, QX7, CX5M Music computer
*KORG	SQD-1
*CASIO	SZ-1
*LINN	Linn Sequencer
*AKAI	ME-20A
*INDUS SYSTEMS	MIDI Dj

PITCH TO MIDI CONVERTERS

*FAIRLIGHT	Voicetracker
*CHERRY LANE	Pitchrider 4000, Pitchrider 7000
*GENTLE ELECTRIC	Model 101 Pitch and Envelope Follower

MIDI GUITARS

*ROLAND
GR 700, PG 200, GR 707,
G-505, G-202, G-808, G-303,
GR 77B, G-77, G-88, G-33

*IBANEZ
Advanced string bend

*OCTAVE PLATEAU
Voyetra MIDI

*SYNTHAXE

MIDI DRUM MACHINES

*ROLAND
TR909

*E-MU
Drumulator, SP-12

*YAMAHA
RX11, RX15, RX21

*SEQUENTIAL CIRCUITS
Drumtracks

*LINN
Linn 9000, Linn Drum Midistudio

*J.L. COOPER
Sound Chest II

*DYNACORD
Percuter-S, Big Brain, Boomer

*CASIO
RZ-1

*WERSI
CX-5

*SIMMONS
SDS9, SDS EPB

*ROLAND
Pad-8 Octapad, DDR-30,
PD-10, PD-20

*OBERHEIM   DX

MIDI SAMPLERS

*ENSONIQ	Mirage, Mirage Digital Multi-Sampler
*AKAI	S612
*DECILLIONIX	DX-1, MIDI-Madness
*SEQUENTIAL	Prophet 2000
*KORG	SDD-2000, SG-1, DSS-1
*PPG WAVE	Waveterm, Waveterm B,
*E-MU	Emulator II
*EUROPA TECHNOLOGIES	Swiss MDB Window Recorder
*FAIRLIGHT	CMI
*SYNCLAVIER	Expandable
*KURZWEIL	250, 250 Expandable, Sound Modeling Program, Sound Block A, MacAttach

MIDI PIANOS AND ORGANS

*KAWAI	EP308M, EP705M, KX series, 1000, 2000, 5000

*YAMAHA	CP70M, CP80M, CP60M
*KORG	MPK-130
*WERSI	Alpha DX3505

MIDI EXPANDER MODULES

*ROLAND	MKS-7 Super Quartet, EM-101 Sound Plus, MKS-20 Digital Piano Sound Module, MKS-80 Super Jupiter, MPG-80, MKS-30 Planet S, MKS-10 Planet P, DDR-30
*360 SYSTEMS	MIDI Bass
*KORG	MR-16
*OBERHEIM	Xpander

MIDI KEYBOARD CONTROLLERS

*KORG	RK-100
*YAMAHA	KX5, KX-1, KX88,
*OBERHEIM	XK
*LYNC	Remote Keyboard
*ROLAND	Axis-1, MKB-200, MKB-300, MKB-1000

*KURZWEIL   MIDI Board

MIDI SYNTHESIZERS

*YAMAHA   CP7, PF10, DX21, DX9, DX7,
                                       DX5, DX1, TX1, TX7, TX216,
                                       TX816 Tone Generator System

*CASIO   CZ-101, CZ-1000, CZ-3000,
                                       CZ-5000, CT-6000

*ROLAND   Juno 106, JX-3P, JX-8P, PG-800,
                                       Jupiter-6, EP50 electronic
                                       piano, Synth Plus-60 (HS-60),
                                       Piano Plus-400 (HP-400), Piano
                                       Plus-300 (HP-300)

*KORG   Poly 61M, Poly 800, Poly
                                       800 Mark II, Ex800 RK-100,
                                       DW 6000, DW 8000, EX 8000

*SEQUENTIAL CIRCUITS   Six Trak, Max, Multi-Trak,

                                       Plus-300 (HP-300)

*KORG   Poly 61M, Poly 800, Poly
                                       800 Mark II, Ex800 RK-100,
                                       DW 6000, DW 8000, EX 8000

*SEQUENTIAL CIRCUITS   Six Trak, Max, Multi-Trak,
                                       Prophet 600, Split-8

*EUROPA   Oscar

*FENDER	Chroma Polaris
*OBERHEIM	Matrix-6, Xpander, OB-8 Matrix-12
*DIGITAL KEYBOARDS	Synergy
*P.P.G. WAVE	Wave 2.3, PRK
*TECHNICS KAWAI	SX-K350, SX-240
*SOLTON	Project 100, Programmer 24, SM 1000
*OCTAVE PLATEAU	Voyetra Eight
*AKAI	AX-80
*BIT	One
*SUZUKI	Keyman
*SIEL	MK-490, MK-610, PX-JR, DK-
*HOHNER	PK250
*SEIKO	DS-250, DS-310
*WERSI	MK-1, Condor
*MOOG	Memory Moog Plus

RECOMMENDED MAGAZINES

BASS PLAYER
Miller Freeman Publications

BYTE
McGraw Hill, Inc.

COMPUTER MUSIC JOURNAL
MIT Press

CD REVIEW
Connell Communications, Inc.

ELECTRONIC MUSICIAN
Mix Publications

FUTURE MUSIC
Key Audio Systems, Ltd.

GUITAR PLAYER
Miller Freeman Publications

HOME OFFICE COMPUTING
Scholastic, Inc.

KEYBOARD MAGAZINE
GPI Publications

MACUSER
Ziff-Davis, Publishing Co.

MCS: MUSIC, COMPUTERS & SOFTWARE
Music, Computers and Software, Inc.

MIX
PBA International

MODERN DRUMMER
Modern Drummer Publications

MUSICIAN
Billboard Publications

MUSIC TECHNOLOGY
Music Makers Publications

PC COMPUTING
Ziff-Davis Publishing Company

PC MAGAZINE
Ziff-Davis Publishing Company

PERSONAL COMPUTING
VNU Business Publications

STEREOPHILE
Larry Archibald Publications

THE ABSOLUTE SOUND
Pearson Publishing

VIDEO REVIEW
Viare Publishing Company

BIBLIOGRAPHY

Alkin, Glyn. TV SOUND OPERATIONS.
London, England: Focal Press, 1975.

Alten, Stanley. AUDIOIN MEDIA.
Belmont, CA: Wadsworth Pub., 1981.

Anderton, Craig. ELECTRONIC PROJECTS FOR MUSICIANS. Saratoga,
CA: Guitar Player Books, 1980.

Anderton, Craig. HOME RECORDING FOR MUSICIANS. Saratoga,
CA: Guitar Player Books, 1978.

Anderton, Craig. MIDI FOR MUSICIANS.
New York, NY: Amsco Publications, 1986.

Anderton, Craig. THE ELECTRONIC MUSICIAN'S DICTIONARY.
New York, NY: Amsco Publications, 1988.

Anderson, Gary. VIDEO EDITING.
White Plains, NY: Knowledge Industry Publications, 1984.

Appleton, Jon H. and Perera, Ronald C. THE DEVELOPMENT AND
PRACTICE OF ELECTRONIC MUSIC. Englewood Cliffs, NJ: Prentice-
Hall, Inc., 1975.

Armbruster, Greg (Ed.) and Darter, Tom (Compiler). THE ART OF
ELECTRONIC MUSIC. New York, NY: GPI Books, 1984.

Backus, John. THE ACOUSTICAL FOUNDATIONS OF MUSIC.
New York, NY: W.W. Norton and Co., 1977.

Bacon, Tony (Ed.). ROCK HARDWARE. New York, NY: Harmony
Books, 1981.

Baird, Jock. UNDERSTANDING MIDI. London, England: Wise Publications, 1986.

Baskerville, David. MUSIC BUSINESS HANDBOOK AN CAREER GUIDE. Los Angeles, CA: The Sherwood Company, 1979.

Bateman, Wayne. INTRODUCTION TO COMPUTER MUSIC. New York, NY: Wiley, 1980.

Beauchamp, J. W., and Von Foerster, H. (Eds.). MUSIC BY COMPUTERS. New York, NY: Wiley, 1969.

Beckwith, John, and Kasamets, Udo, (Eds.). THE MODERN COMPOSER AND HIS WORLD. Toronto, Canada: University of Toronto Press, 1961.

Bjorneberg, Paul (Ed.). MUSIC USA 86. Chicago, IL: American Music Conference, 1986.

Bjorneberg, Paul (Ed.). MUSIC USA 89. Chicago, IL: American Music Conference, 1989.

Boom, Michael. MUSIC THROUGH MIDI. Redmond, WA: Microsoft Press, 1987.

Borwick John (Ed.). SOUND RECORDING PRACTICE. Oxford, England: Oxford University Press, 1980.

Buban and Schmitt. UNDERSTANDING ELECTRICITY AND ELEC-TRONICS. New York, NY: McGraw-Hill, 1969.

Campbell, Russell. PHOTOGRAPHIC THEORY FOR THE MOTION PICTURE CAMERAMAN. London, England: Zwemmer, 1970.

Carlson, Vance and Sylvia. THE PROFESSIONAL LIGHTING HAND-BOOK. New York, NY: Verlan Industries, 1967.

Cetron, Marvin and Davies, Owen. AMERICAN RENAISSANCE: OUR LIFE AT THE TURN OF THE 21st CENTURY. New York, NY: St. Martin's Press, 1989

Chamberlin, Hal. MUSICAL APPLICATIONS OF MICROPROCES-SORS. Rochelle Park, NJ: Hayden Book Company, Inc., 1980.

Cope, David. NEW DIRECTIONS IN MUSIC. Dubuque, IA: Wm. C. Brown Co., 1971.

Crombie, David. THE NEW COMPLETE SYNTHESIZER. London, England: Omnibus Press, 1986.

Cross, Lowell. A BIBLIOGRAPHY OF ELECTRONIC MUSIC. Toronto, Canada: University of Toronto Press, 1966.

Crowhurst, Norman H. ELECTRONIC MUSICAL INSTRUMENTS. Blue Ridge Summit, PA: Tab Books, 1977.

Davies, Hugh. INTERNATIONAL ELECTRONIC MUSIC CATALOG. Cambridge, MA: M.I.T. Press, 1968.

Davis, D. and Davis, C. SOUND SYSTEM ENGINEERING. Indianapo-lis, IN: Howard Sams & Co., 1974.

Deutsch, Herbert A. SYNTHESIS. Alfred, NY, 1976.

Devarahi. THE COMPLETE GUIDE TO SYNTHESIZERS. Englewood Cliffs, NJ: Prentice-Hall, 1982.

Dolan, Robert Emmett. MUSIC IN MODERN MEDIA. New York, NY: G. Schirmer, 1967.

Douglas, Alan. ELECTRONIC MUSIC PRODUCTION. London, England: Pitman, 1973.

Douglas, Alan. THE ELECTRONIC MUSICAL INSTRUMENT MANUAL. London, England: Pitman, 1968.

Eargle, John. HANDBOOK OF RECORDING ENGINEERING. New York, NY: Van Nostrand Reinhold, 1986.

Eaton, M.L. ELECTRONIC MUSIC; A HANDBOOK OF SOUND SYNTHESIS AND CONTROL. Kansas City, MO; Orcus Publications, 1969.

Fink, D.G. (Ed.). COLOR TEVEVISION STANDARDS. New York, NY: McGraw-Hill, 1955.

Fink, Robert and Ricci, Robert. THE LANGUAGE OF TWENTIETH CENTURY MUSIC. New York, NY: Schirmer Books, 1975.

Flatt, Jane D. (Pub.). THE WORLD ALMANAC AND BOOKS OF FACTS - 1985. New York, NY: Newspaper Enterprise Association Inc., 1984.

Friedman, Dean. THE COMPLETE GUIDE TO SYNTHESIZERS, SEQUENCERS & DRUM MACHINES. New York, NY: Amsco Publications, 1985.

Griffiths, Paul. A GUIDE TO ELECTRONIC MUSIC. London, England: Thames and Hudson, 1980.

Gross, L.S. THE NEW TELEVISION TECHNOLOGIES. Debuque, IA: William Brown, 1983.

Hagen, Earle. SCORING FOR FILMS. New York, NY: E.D.J. Music, 1971.

Hall, Donald. MUSICAL ACOUSTICS.
Belmont, CA: Wadsworth, 1980.

Hammond, Ray. THE MUSICIAN AND THE MICRO.
Poole, Dorset, England: Blandford Press, 1983.

Hiller, Lajaren A., Jr., and Isaacson, Leonard M. EXPERIMENTAL MUSIC: COMPOSITION WITH AN ELECTRONIC COMPUTER. New York, NY: McGraw-Hill, 1959.

Holmes, Thomas B. ELECTRONIC AND EXPERIMENTAL MUSIC. New York, NY: Charles Scribner's Sons, 1985.

Horn, Delton T. ELECTRONIC MUSIC SYNTHESIZERS. Blue Ridge Sumlmit, PA: Tab Books, 1980.

Hurtig, Brent (Ed.). SYNTHESIZERS AND COMPUTERS. Milwaukee, WI: Hal Leonard Publishing Company, 1987.

Hutchins, Bernie. MUSICAL ENGINEER'S HANDBOOK. New York, NY: Electronotes, 1975.

Johnson, George. MACHINERY OF THE MIND: INSIDE THE NEW SCIENCE OF ARTIFICIAL INTELLIGENCE. Redmond, WA: Tempus, 1986.

Jordan, Thurston. GLOSSARY OF MOTION PICTURE TERMINOLOGY. Menlo Park, CA: Pacific Coast, 1968.

Judd, F. C. ELECTRONIC MUSIC AND MUSIQUE CONCRETE. London, England: Neville Spearman, 1961.

Judd, F. C. ELECTRONICS IN MUSIC. London, England: Spearman, 1972.

Kirby, Michael. FUTURIST PERFORMANCE. New York, NY: Dutton, 1971.

Lambert, Dennis & Zalkind. PRODUCING HIT RECORDS. New York, NY: Schirmer, 1980.

Lazendorf, Peter. THE VIDEOTAPING HANDBOOK. New York, NY: Harmony Press, 1983.

189

Lee, William. BELWIN DICTIONARY OF MUSIC. Miami, FL: Belwin Mills Publishing Corp., 1994.

Lefkoff, Gerald (Ed.). COMPUTER APPLICATIONS IN MUSIC. Morgantown, WV: West Virginia University Library, 1967.

Lincoln, Harry B. (Ed.). THE COMPUTER AND MUSIC. Ithaca, NY: Cornell University Press, 1970.

London, Kurt. FILM MUSIC. London, England: Faber & Faber, 1970.

Mackay, Andy. ELECTRONIC MUSIC: THE INSTRUMENTS, MUSIC AND MUSICIANS. Minneapolis, MN: Control Data, 1981.

Martin, George (Ed.). MAKING MUSIC. London, England: Pan Books, Ltd, 1983.

Massey, Howard. THE COMPLETE DX711. New York, NY: Amsco Publications, 1987.

Mathews, Max V. TECHNOLOGY OF COMPUTER MUSIC. Cambridge, MS: M.I.T. Press, 1969.

Miller, Fred. STUDIO RECORDING FOR MUSICIANS. New York, NY: Amsco Publications, 1981.

Nakajima, H., Doi, T.T., Fukuda, J., Iga, A. DIGITAL AUDIO TECHNOLOGY. Blue Ridge, PA: Tab Books, 1983.

Oppenheim, A.V. DIGITAL SIGNAL PROCESSING. Englewood Cliffs, NJ: Prentice-Hall, 1975.

Pohlmann, Ken C. PRINCIPLES OF DIGITAL AUDIO. Indianapolis, IN: Howard Sams, 1985.

Porter, Kent. THE NEW AMERICAN COMPUTER DICTIONARY. New York, NY: Signet Books, 1985.

Prenis, John. THE COMPUTER DICTIONARY. Philadelphia, PA: Running Press, 1983.

Reichardt, Jasia. CYBERNETIC SERENDIPITY: THE COMPUTER AND THE ARTS. New York, NY: Praeger, 1969.

Roads, Curtis (Ed.). COMPOSERS AND THE COMPUTER. Los Altos, CA: William Kaufmann, Inc., 1985.

Roads, Curtis and Strawn, John (Ed.s) FOUNDATIONS OF COMPUTER MUSIC. Cambridge, MA: MIT Press, 1985.

Rodgers, Harold A. DICTIONARY OF DATA PROCESSING TERMS. New York, NY: Funk & Wagnalls, 1970.

Roederer, Juan. INTRODUCTION TO THE PHYSICS AND PSYCHOPHYSICS OF MUSIC (Second Edition). New York, NY: Springer-Verlag, 1979

Rona, Jeff. MIDI: THE INS, OUTS & THRUS. Milwaukee, WI: Hal Leonard Books, 1987.

Rossing, Thomas. THE SCIENCE OF SOUND. Reading, MA: Addison-Wesley, 1982.

Sadie, Stanley (Ed.). THE NEW GROVE DICTIONARY OF MUSICAL INSTRUMENTS (Three volumes). London, England: Macmillan Press, 1984.

Schafer, R. Murray. THE TUNING OF THE WORLD. New York, NY: Knopf, 1977.

Schwartz, Elliott S. ELECTRONIC MUSIC: A LISTENER'S GUIDE. New York, NY: Praeger, 1973.

Shea, Richard P. AMPLIFIER HANDBOOK. New York, NY: McGraw-Hill, 1968.

Shemel, Sidney & Krasilovsky, M. William. THIS BUSINESS OF MUSIC. New York, NY: Billboard, 1979.

Strange, Allen. ELECTRONIC MUSIC: SYSTEMS, TECHNIQUES AND CONTROLS. Dubuque, IA: William C. Brown, 1972.

Strawn, John. DIGITAL AUDIO SIGNAL PROCESSING. Los Altos, CA: Kaufmann, 1985.

Tjepkema, Sandra L. A BIBLIOGRAPHY OF COMPUTER MUSIC. Iowa City, IA: University of Iowa Press, 1981.

Tobler, John & Grundy, Stuart. THE RECORD PRODUCERS. London, England: BBC, 1982.

Traylor, J.G. PHYSICS OF STEREO-QUAD SOUND. Iowa City, IA: Iowa State University Press, 1977.

Tremaine, Howard M. THE AUDIO CYCLOPEDIA. Indianapolis, IN: Howard W. Sams, 1974.

Trythall, Gilbert. PRINCIPLES AND PRACTICE OF ELECTRONIC MUSIC. New York, NY: Grosset & Dunlap, 1974.

Wadhams, Wayne. DICTIONARY OF MUSIC PRODUCTION & ENGINEERING TERMINOLOGY. New York, NY: Schirmer Books, 1988.

White, Gordon. VIDEO RECORDING. Boston, MA: Butterworth, 1972.

White, Gordon. VIDEO TECHNIQUES. Boston, MA: Butterworth, 1982.

Winckel, Fritz. MUSIC, SOUND AND SENSATION. New York, NY: Dover, 1967.

Woram, John M. THE RECORDING STUDIO HANDBOOK. Plainview, NY: ELAR Publishing Company, Inc., 1982.

Zettl, Herbert. TELEVISION PRODUCTION HANDBOOK. Belmont, CA: Wadsworth, 1984.